Journey Toward Independence

Etching, circa 1916, of King's Chapel on the corner of
Tremont and School Streets in Boston, MA.

Journey Toward Independence

King's Chapel's Transition to Unitarianism

Carl Scovel and Charles C. Forman
The 1989 Minns Lecture

Skinner House Books • Boston

Published by Skinner House Books, an imprint of the Unitarian
Universalist Association, 25 Beacon St., Boston, MA 02108

Every attempt has been made to avoid sexist and racist language in this
book. When used in direct quotation, however, documents have been left
unchanged for historical accuracy.

BX
98&1
.B74
S36
1993

ISBN 1-55896-310-3
Printed in U.S.A.

99 98 97 96 95 94 93
10 9 8 7 6 5 4 3 2 1

Project Editor: Brenda Wong
Copyeditor: Linda Hotchkiss Mehta
Designer: Suzanne Morgan

Library of Congress Cataloging-in-Publication Data

Scovel, Carl, 1932-
    Journey toward independence : King's Chapel's transition to
Unitarianism : the 1989 Minns lecture / by Carl Scovel and Charles
C. Forman.
        p.   cm.
    Includes bibliographical references.
    Contents: Rational religion in England and New England on the
eve of the American Revolution / Charles C. Forman — James Free-
man, an Enlightenment Christian ; Without benefit of clergy / Carl R.
Scovel — King's Chapel, transition toward Unitarianism / Charles C.
Forman.
    ISBN 1-55896-310-3
    1. King's Chapel (Boston, Mass.)—History. 2. Boston (Mass.)—
Church history. 3. Massachusetts—Church history. 4. Anglican
Communion—Massachusetts—Boston—History. 5. Unitarianism—
Massachusetts—Boston—History. I. Forman, Charles C. (Charles
Conrad), 1926- . II. Title. III. Title: Minns Lecture.
    BX9861.B74S36 1993
    289. 1'74461—dc20
                                              93-13829
                                              CIP

Contents

Journey Toward Independence

Rational Religion in England and New England on the Eve of the American Revolution

How eighteenth-century Anglican tolerance with its emphasis on morality, duty, and virtue nourished liberal attitudes in the churches of New England.

———————————◆•◆———————————

These Minns Lectures are an account of how the first Anglican church in New England became the first Unitarian church in America. In 1986 the congregation of King's Chapel celebrated the 300th anniversary of the establishing of King's Chapel as an Anglican congregation in Puritan Boston. In 1987 it marked the 200th anniversary of the ordination of James Freeman. This ordination was the culminating act in a series of events that made King's Chapel the first Unitarian church in America.

It is noteworthy that the two churches administering the Minns Lectureship, the First Church in Boston, gathered in 1630 as a staunch bulwark of Puritanism and the Congregational Way, and King's Chapel, the church of the Anglican congregation of 1686, should today be sister churches within the Unitarian Universalist Association. History's ways are strange indeed, but in this instance perhaps not as strange as they may first appear.

Both churches are children of the seventeenth-century Church of England. That century was marked by bitter controversies that ultimately led to divisions within Anglicanism. Let us look briefly at events in the life of the Church of England after its break with Rome. Henry VIII (1491-1547) was given the title, "Defender of the Faith" in 1521 for writing a book defending the Catholic understanding of the seven sacraments against Luther's newly published sacramental theories. Twelve years later his marriage to Catherine was dissolved by the action of Archbishop Cranmer, clearing the way for Henry's marriage to Anne Boleyn, and thus effectively separating the Church of England from the Church of Rome.

Nevertheless, when Henry died in 1547 the Church of England was in most ways "catholic" still in thought and feeling. There were two distinguishing points of utmost importance: papal authority had been set aside, and the language of the liturgy was English.

Edward VI, son of Jane Seymour, came to the throne when he was ten years old. His education had been, and continued to be, in the hands of men of reformed sympathy so that the liturgy and theology of the Church of England moved rapidly toward a reformation according to Calvinistic ideas. An event of monumental significance was the publication of the *Book of Common Prayer* in 1549. Edward's untimely death brought his half-sister Mary Tudor to the throne in 1553. She set about at once to make England Roman Catholic again, and in the process earned the nickname "Bloody Mary." Her cause was not destined to succeed, but for five years she prevailed, sending Thomas Cranmer, archbishop of Canterbury, and a host of clergy numbering some 300 to burn at the stake as martyrs to the cause of the English Reformation.

When Elizabeth I (1533-1603) came to the throne in 1558, the religious question was the central problem of the realm. To have been first Roman, then Reformed, then Roman again, and now once more Protestant—all within a quarter of a century—could only have produced chaos and confusion on every side. England was largely Catholic in sentiment, but there was, especially among its leaders, a strong Calvinistic presence; Elizabeth distrusted both.

Matthew Parker became the Queen's archbishop and, under his careful guidance, uniformity was gradually achieved. What emerged was the "via media" of Anglicanism. Conformity with comprehension was the rule in which the broadest possible range of opinion could be accommodated within the church, united by a common liturgy and common practice. The Church of England thus set for itself a difficult ideal; it would be at once "catholic and reformed."

During the seventeenth century, people attempted to translate that ideal into a reality. The Puritans who had of necessity accommodated themselves to the principles of the Elizabethan settlement in religion hoped for greater opportunity to work with Elizabeth's successor for further reform in liturgy and practice along Protestant lines. James the First came to the throne in 1603 and promptly put the Puritans on notice when, at the Hampton Court Conference the following year, he declared that the Puritans would conform "else he would harry them out of the land." What came of that is another story we cannot follow here.

One event of singular importance must be noted here, namely the appearance of the Authorized or King James Version of the Bible in 1611. It provided English-speaking Christianity with the greatest single instrument for the shaping of its liturgical language as a vehicle for articulating the deepest emotions of piety and worship.

When Charles I came to the throne in 1625, he found to his satisfaction considerable anti-Calvinist sentiment. Thus encouraged, he supported movements within the church for rediscovering and reappropriating the Catholic elements in Anglicanism. Thus was the high church born (not to be identified with the Oxford Movement of the Nineteenth Century) that would dominate the Caroline Church of Charles I and Charles II and give rise to the golden age of Anglican spirituality.

Time does not permit us to consider the impact of the Civil Wars, the execution of Charles the First, and the stormy period of Cromwell's Commonwealth on the life of the Church of England. It must suffice to say that with the Restoration in 1660 there was inevitably a reaction against the Puritan party, ushering in a new period of enforced conformity (cf. the Act of Conformity of 1662) and a new chapter in the history of English dissent. Only with the reigns of William and Mary

(1689-1702) and of Anne (1702-1714) at the turn of the century does the Church of England enter into a time of relative calm.

When we look at the eighteenth century, we are aware of a different mood; it is an age in which tolerance and rational religion come into their own. One can see the priorities of the age by looking at a typical Anglican church of the period. That sermons were emphasized more than Holy Communion is evident, for the pulpit and the reading desk were the focal points, usually combined with a clerk's desk (hence the three-decker pulpits), and complete with sounding board and pulpit cushions. (The cushions are gone, but otherwise King's Chapel's pulpit is a splendid example of the type.) Holy Communion was usually celebrated three or four times a year. The liturgy was marked by order and quiet routine; enthusiasm and any display of fervor were to be distrusted. The sermon was a carefully reasoned essay showing little interest in theology, stressing instead themes of morality and virtue. The age of reason had indeed arrived; it was everywhere evident in the mood and practice of the English churches.

Who were the persons and what were the intellectual movements that shaped the age? In the seventeenth century the Cambridge Platonists had argued that reason supported natural and revealed religion and stood for both tolerance and comprehension within the Church of England. The Latitudinarians gave little attention to dogma and cared less for any careful observance of the rubrics directing liturgical practice. They tended to be Arminian in theology, stressing the freedom of the will as opposed to Calvinistic theories of determinism, and affirmed the effectiveness of Christ's sacrifice for all, and not alone the Elect. Reason and scripture were the sources of revelation and authority; by these principles, it was believed, a truly "catholic Christianity" might be promoted.

Deism, too, made a deep impression on the thought of the eighteenth century. Deism is a system of natural religion that stresses belief in a Supreme Being who is architect and creator of the universe, who is worthy of worship, and who is best worshiped by virtuous deeds.

Eighteenth-century Christians saw further evidence of God's presence chiefly in a kind of Divine Providence at work within the natural order. Morality, duty, and virtue are key notions. Horton Davies gives us a delightful extract from the writings of one of the deist clergy and a great favorite of the time, Archbishop Tillotson:

> No other age would surely have presumed to give Jesus Christ a testimonial of good character, or so deftly remove the "scandal" of the Cross from the record. Here is Tillotsons urbane portrait of the founder of Christianity: "The Virtues of his Life are pure, without any Mixture of Infirmity and Imperfection. He had Humility without any Meanness of Spirit; Innocency without Weakness; Wisdom without Cunning; and Constancy and Resolution in that which was good, without Stiffness of Conceit and peremptoriness of Humour: In a word, his Virtues were shining without Vanity, Heroical without anything of transport, and very extraordinary without being in the least extravagant."[1]

Arminianism steadily gained ground during the reign of Queen Anne. It may, indeed, have prepared the way for a controversy that arose during the latter years of her reign that would set the theological agenda for the century.[2] Of all those belonging to the Arminian party, one person of singular distinction stands out. I refer to Samuel Clarke, important for his theological and liturgical interests to the subsequent history of King's Chapel. In time, he came to be a mentor to leaders of both English and American Unitarianism.

Samuel Clarke (1675-1729), a graduate of Caius College, Cambridge, and an Anglican divine, early gained a reputation for scholarly pursuits. As Boyle Lecturer in 1704 and 1705, he took for his theme the defense of rational theology under the formidable title, "A Discourse Concerning the Being and Attributes of God, the Obligations of Natural Religion, and the Truth and Certainty of the Christian Revelation." In 1709 he became Rector of St. James Piccadilly, and there in 1712 he wrote *Scripture-Doctrine of the Trinity* in which he collected texts relating to the Trinity, gave a statement of the doctrine, and reviewed trinitarian passages in the *Book of Common Prayer*. He was said to be an Arian.

Although the label "Arian" is a reference to the fourth-century view that the Son was created and is therefore not equal to God the Father, eighteenth-century English Arians were simply radical Arminians who stressed reason and scripture as the full and sufficient source of authority. Their examination of scripture convinced them that any doctrine of the Trinity or of the deity of Christ in the orthodox sense was absent from the New Testament. Such doctrines were not to be found in the teachings of Christ or the apostles, and so were not necessary for salvation.

F. J. Powicke gives a good account of nonconformist Arians, and his description may generally be applied to those of the Arian party within Anglicanism as well. They had complete faith in God's reasonableness, and therefore revelation and reason could never be in conflict.[3] Samuel Clarke declared: "That which is truly the Law of Nature . . . is in like manner the Will of God." And again, "Moral Virtue is the essence of the Life of all true Religion."[4]

Tillotson and Clarke must be seen as but two thinkers representative of an age in which the several sources of rational religion came together to create a climate within the Anglican church that provides a context in which to understand the particular history of King's Chapel. Let us now turn to examine evidence for the growth of rational religion in the churches of New England on the eve of the American Revolution.

In the seventeenth century the churches of the New England Way worked out their polity, that is, their way of organization and governance. The Pilgrims arriving in Plymouth in 1620 were self-avowed Separatists, while the Puritans of Salem and Boston still thought of themselves as members of the Church of England, albeit committed to the Puritan agenda of reform.

Within a few years the distinction was moot: the Puritan churches became *de facto* Separatist, and the Pilgrim churches formed ties with them. In 1648—eighteen years after the First Church in Boston was gathered—the Cambridge Synod was convened and from that historic synod came the Cambridge Platform, adopted (after intense discussion) by the vote of some fifty churches. The Platform set forth the theology of the Church and its ordering, thus articulating the essential character of the churches of the New England Way. Between 1657 and 1662 the Half Way Covenant was adopted, relaxing the requirements for baptism and so preparing the way for the twofold system of church and parish. Thus the Puritan ideal of the Church as the gathered body of saints by election and calling began its evolution.

The distinguishing mark of the New England Church was its covenant as the basis of Christian community. The sign of the gathered church was the company of those joined together by a covenant, not a creed. The Salem Covenant of 1629 provides a clear model:

> We covenant with the Lord, and one with another, and do bind ourselves in the presence of God, to walk together in all His ways, according as he is pleased to reveal himself unto us in his blessed Word of Truth.

It is a statement of resolve, not of dogma. Notice its beginning: not "I believe. . . ." but "We covenant with the Lord. . . ."!

The New England Way in church order was a unique experiment and one that was destined to hold sway for fully two centuries in what emerged in Massachusetts as the Congregational establishment. The struggle for full civil freedom for dissenters of the Congregational establishment continued from the middle of the century until it was finally resolved by the Toleration Act signed by William and Mary in 1689, three years after the founding of King's Chapel.

As in England, so in New England, the church of the eighteenth century is marked by a concern for order. This feeling for order on the part of the churches assigned special importance to the notion of a settled ministry, and life settle-

ments were not uncommon. With settlement went the guaran-
tee of the freedom of the pulpit, thus contributing to a struc-
ture that provided for continuity while at the same time allow-
ing for gradual change in theological thought and practice.

By the end of the century the great majority of the oldest
parishes in Eastern New England had abandoned Calvinist
thought for a kind of rational Christianity, touched by deism,
and holding to an Arian christology based on the authority of
the New Testament.

I can think of no event that better illustrates the theological
climate of New England at the middle of the eighteenth
century than can be seen in the founding of the Dudlean
Lectureship at Harvard College in 1751. By the terms of his
bequest, Chief Justice Paul Dudley directed that there be
delivered an annual lecture on a series of topics including
natural religion, revealed religion, the validity of nonepiscopal
ordination, and the errors of Popery. (The last was dropped
from the series at the beginning of this century.) The topics
admirably articulate the theological interest of both the moderate Calvinist party and those of the liberals of the day,
whether Arminian or deist. Scripture and reason were regarded as complementary rather than antithetical sources of
revelation in the minds of both groups.

The Calvinist relied on revelation, but that revelation could
be examined and confirmed by rational means. The liberals, by
the same token, claimed that reason was a sufficient guide in
discovering the will of God, albeit enhanced and supported by
the revelation contained in Scripture.[5]

The thought of two men is seminal in understanding the
influences that shaped the thinking of these liberals: Samuel
Clarke, already mentioned, and John Locke (1632-1704), a
staunch defender of toleration and free inquiry in matters of
religion. His most influential work was *The Reasonableness of
Christianity as Delivered in the Scriptures*, which appeared in
1695 and which was being read in New England by both
students and clergy soon after its publication.

Of those who may be regarded as most influential among
the liberal Christian clergy of the period, three men may be

mentioned. The first is Ebenezer Gay (1696-1787), for seventy years minister of the First Parish, the Old Ship Church of Hingham.[6] Gay's ministry provides us as convincing an example as any of the principle of the free pulpit. An ardent Tory preaching to a congregation overwhelmingly committed to the cause of American independence, his prayers at every Sunday service during the revolutionary war included fervent intercessions for the victory of the King's soldiers. He was as staunchly liberal in his theology as he was conservative in his politics. Gay opposed all creeds and called for freedom of inquiry in religion. Reason will confirm every true theological claim, he declared, and argued that an absurd doctrine is not of God. Like others of his generation, he held that in nature one found clear evidences of a First Cause. Furthermore, the study of nature reveals a universe in which order and harmony reflect the true character of its Creator. The Creator is omniscient, omnipotent, and benevolent.

The second is Charles Chauncy (1704-1787), for sixty years minister of Boston's First Church.[7] Like his contemporary and close friend Ebenezer Gay, he was a rationalist in religion. Above all else Chauncy dreaded emotionalism and enthusiasm in religion, which he saw disrupting the life of the churches in the period that followed the Great Awakening. Religious enthusiasm, he argued, is more likely to be attributed to an excessive imagination or some kind of madness than an authentic experience of God. The Holy Spirit works through the rational faculties in bringing men and women to a true understanding of religious truth. Like Gay, Chauncy stressed the notion of Divine Providence, one of the touchstones of Christian faith in the eighteenth century.

Finally, there was Jonathan Mayhew (1720-1766), the son of Increase Mayhew, missionary to the Indians of Martha's Vineyard. Mayhew, considerably younger than Gay and Chauncy, was minister of the prestigious West Church from 1747 until his early death in 1766. His orthodoxy was suspect in some quarters from the very beginning of his ministry, so that ministers of the Boston churches were not invited to his ordination. His congregation invited, instead, clergy from the surrounding towns. To be sure, Ebenezer Gay was there and preached the ordination sermon.

Mayhew's closest friends included both Gay and Chauncy, and like them he subscribed to the general body of Arminian theological opinion. He acknowledged the influence of Samuel Clarke in his thinking and was more explicitly rationalist than either of his older friends. Mayhew denied the doctrine of the Fall and the resultant impairment of human nature out of hand. Like Chauncy and Gay, he held a theological anthropology that attributed to human nature a moral endowment that enabled men and women to distinguish good and evil. In our moral nature, he said, we resemble God.

Although Mayhew stood somewhat apart from his fellow clergy (a fact confirmed by his not joining in the widespread practice among the churches of monthly pulpit exchanges) and is certainly to be placed in the vanguard of advanced Arminian thought, on the issues of independency he stood shoulder to shoulder with his colleagues.

Episcopacy was, for him, an unmitigated evil, and he vigorously opposed any effort to introduce Anglican bishops into the American colonies. One of the ironies of the history of the liberal movement in New England vis-a-vis King's Chapel did not go unnoticed by the historian G. Adolf Koch who wrote: "Such is the beauty of fate, indeed, that the Church of England which was Mayhew's particular *bete noir* was to give America its first Unitarian Church."[8]

For all the fears of Mayhew and his congregational brethren relative to episcopacy, the Arminian party owed a considerable debt to the liberals within the Anglican church. The extent of that debt needs to be better known in identifying the influences that gave rise to the Arianism that emerged in the churches of New England near the middle of the century.

The views of Thomas Hutchinson, Royal Governor from 1771-1774 and a great-grandson of none other than Anne Hutchinson, may be typical of the religious sentiments of a growing number of men and women in the Boston of his time. I quote from his biographer Thomas Bailyn:

A true religious life to Hutchinson meant simply the
worship of God and rectitude. He judged the practice of
religion by its results, in human terms: "the longer I live
the less stress I lay upon modes and forms of religion,
and I do not love a good man the less because he and I are
not of just the same way of thinking." For himself he
certainly would have chosen the Anglican church if he
had the opportunity to choose; had "he been born and
bred there," he wrote Bernard in 1771, "I would never
have left it for any other communion." Its rational, toler-
ant views were his own, and he could see no particular
objection to the establishment of an American episcopate
if its jurisdiction were limited to the spiritual lives of
Anglicans.[9]

But, says Bailyn, he remained in the Congregational Church
(the New Brick was the family church), although he was closer
to the rationalist Andrew Eliot and Henry Caner of King's
Chapel where he frequently worshiped.

I think of two examples familiar to most of us that express
the piety and spirit of the age we have been considering. The
first is George Washington's prayer for our country. Now,
fortunately, it may be found in the King's Chapel prayerbook.

Almighty God, we make our earnest prayer that thou wilt
keep the United States in thy holy protection; that thou
wilt incline the hearts of the citizens to cultivate a spirit
of subordination and obedience to the government, and
entertain a brotherly affection and love for one another
and for their fellow citizens of the United States at large.
And finally, that thou wilt most graciously be pleased to
dispose us all to do justice, to love mercy, and to demean
ourselves with that charity, humility, and pacific temper
of mind which were the characteristics of the divine
author of our blessed religion, and without a humble
imitation of whose example in these things we can never
hope to be a happy nation. Amen.[10]

The second example is the magnificent hymn in praise of the Creator by the Anglican poet and essayist, Joseph Addison, and found in *Hymns of the Spirit*:

> The spacious firmament on high,
>   With all the blue ethereal sky,
> And spangled heav'ns, a shining frame,
>   Their great Original proclaim.
>
> The unwearied sun from day to day
>   Does his Creator's pow'r display,
> And publishes to ev'ry land
>   The work of an almighty hand.
>
> Soon as the evening shades prevail
>   The moon takes up the wondrous tale,
> And nightly to the list'ning earth
>   Repeats the story of her birth;
>
> Whilst all the stars that round her burn
>   And all the planets in their turn,
> Confirm the tidings as they roll,
>   And spread the truth from pole to pole.
>
> What though in solemn silence all
>   Move round the dark terrestrial ball?
> What tho' no real voice nor sound
>   Amid their radiant orbs be found?
>
> In reason's ear they all rejoice
>   And utter forth a glorious voice,
> Forever singing as they shine,
>   "The hand that made us is divine."

I have attempted to describe how two very different systems, Anglicanism and New England Puritanism, in the course of the eighteenth century gave rise to variant forms of rational Christianity. King's Chapel, rooted in the seventeenth-century Anglicanism but shaped by the special culture that flourished among the churches of the New England Way, found in the second century of its history its own unique identity.

Notes

1. Horton Davies, *Worship and Theology in England, from Watts and Wesley to Maurice, 1690-1850* (Princeton, NJ: Princeton University Press, 1975), p. 56.
2. *Cf.* Roger Thomas's account of this in his article "Presbyterianism in Transition," *Hibbert Journal*, 1962, LX: 195-203.
3. *Cf.* F. J. Powicke's article in *Transactions of the Unitarian Historical Society*, May 1918, *1*(2):101-128.
4. Cited in Basil Wiley, *The Eighteenth Century Background* (Boston: Beacon Press, 1961), p. 60.
5. For an account of supernatural rationalism *cf.* Chapter 6 in Conrad Wright, *The Beginnings of Unitarianism in America* (Boston: Starr King, 1955).
6. For a good recent study of Gay, *cf.* Robert Wilson, *Ebenezer Gay and the Rise of Rational Religion in New England, 1696-1787* (Philadelphia: University of Pennsylvania Press, 1984).
7. For a good recent study of Chauncy, see Charles Lippy, *Seasonable Revolutionary: The Mind of Charles Chauncy* (Chicago: Nelson-Hall, 1981).
8. G. Adolf Koch, *Republican Religion: The American Revolution and the Cult of Reason* (New York: Holt, 1933), p. 203.
9. Thomas Bailyn, *The Ordeal of Thomas Hutchinson* (Cambridge: Harvard, 1974), pp. 22ff.
10. *King's Chapel Prayerbook* (Boston: Peter Edes, 1785), p. 174f.
11. Joseph Addison, *Hymns of the Spirit* (Boston: Beacon Press, 1937)

TWO

James Freeman: An Enlightenment Christian

An account of how James Freeman came to King's Chapel, and how he and the church emended the 1662 Anglican prayerbook.

———— •••• ————

Although earlier historians have claimed that James Freeman alone altered the character and history of King's Chapel, I will argue that he and his congregation were themselves shaped by the events and ideas of their age. James Freeman succeeded because he embodied the chief elements of his culture—Puritan idealism, Enlightenment rationality, Federalist democratic ideals, and a "reasonable" reading of the Christian Bible. He was a man of his time and only as such could he have led his people to a new religious identity.

He was born on April 22, 1759, in Charlestown. His father, Constant, was first a sea captain and then a merchant, who had moved to Charlestown with his wife, Lois, from Truro on Cape Cod four years before James, their oldest, was born. Shortly thereafter they moved to Boston where two more sons and a daughter were born to them.

James Freeman entered the Latin School on School Street (across the street from King's Chapel) when he was seven, and with the aid of rod and repetition learned Greek, Latin, rhetoric, mathematics, and the other rudiments of a liberal education. The founders of this school intended to create obedient students, not realizing that "by equipping their sons with the tools of communication, they . . . [were] breeding debaters and demagogues, radicals and revolutionaries, idealists and icono-clasts."[1] James Freeman grew up to be an educated man equipped with the literary and political skills that would later help him to reform the church that was only a few yards from his classroom.

The Freeman family attended First Church on Cornhill where James's brothers and sisters were baptized and which his parents joined, his mother in 1766. There they heard the great liberal preacher of Boston, Charles Chauncy. Twenty years earlier, Dr. Chauncy had attacked the evangelists of New England's Great Awakening for their emotionalism, and for over a decade he had been writing in secret a treatise on universal salvation.

Charles Chauncy believed that God was above all else be-nevolent. God's benevolence, he said, was "a principle dispos-ing and prompting the communication of happiness." What was good for God was good for God's children. It was their business to be good in order that they might be happy. Moral-ity and holiness were practically the same thing. And, wrote Charles Chauncy in private, someday everyone will be holy and happy. This was the doctrine that Constant and Lois Freeman heard at First Church, and this was the doctrine upon which their four children were suckled.

Armed with a Latin School education and Charles Chauncy's piety, James Freeman went to Harvard College in 1773. He was fourteen, the usual age for admission to that institution. At Harvard, Freeman encountered the intellectual movement known to us as the Enlightenment, a movement closely asso-ciated with the English philosopher John Locke.

In 1686, the very year that King's Chapel was founded, John Locke was in exile in Holland writing his most famous work, modestly titled *An Essay Concerning Human Understanding*. Locke believed that each of us is born with a completely blank mind. Upon this clear slate (literally *tabula rasa*) are inscribed all of our encounters with the world of things, people, and words. The imprint of these encounters upon our minds con-stitutes our knowledge.

We are not born, said Locke, with preconceived ideas, as

Plato argued. What we call "ideas" are simply the mental representation (the record on our mind) of those things, persons, or experiences that we encounter outside of ourselves. The real world, said Locke, is the world "out there," not the world "in there."

Locke assumed that man's chief end was not to glorify and enjoy God (as the *Westminster Shorter Catechism* had it) but to be happy. The right use of reason would make one happy, and all the essential truths of life, discovered through reason, would make happiness inevitable. To us, who live in a world of immense and inexplicable suffering, Locke may seem curiously optimistic (small wonder that Voltaire lampooned such optimism in *Candide*), but to his century Locke brought good news, as heartening as any text from scripture.

With the imminent accession of a new king, Locke returned from Holland to England in 1688 and gratefully wrote a treatise defending constitutional monarchy. It was his philosophical writings, however, which most attracted readers, and particularly a group of Scots who came to be known as "the common-sense school of philosophy." You could almost say that they were anti-philosophical philosophers. "I despise philosophy," said their foremost spokesperson, Thomas Reid, ". . . let my Soul dwell in Common Sense."

These philosophers held that the great truths of human existence were obvious to anyone of moderate intelligence. In fact, once a person heard these truths clearly and simply expounded, he or she would realize that they were "self-evident." We find that in our Declaration of Independence: "We hold these truths to be self-evident, that all men are created equal, that they are endowed by their Creator with certain inalienable rights, that among these rights are life, liberty, and the pursuit of happiness. . . . "

The writers of the Declaration and our Constitution were influenced by the Scottish common-sense philosophers. They too thought that the truth, clearly seen, is simple. For example, no proposition can be both true and false at the same time; or, what we see really *does* exist; or, the laws of nature will operate in the future as they do now. Today we question such axioms, but two centuries ago they were as plain as the nose on one's face, assuming that one believed it was really there.

Anglican theologians used the work of the Scottish philosophers and used it to buttress the claims of Christian faith, and these were the theologians who were read by seminarians at Harvard College in the 1770s: Archbishop Tillotson, Bishop Butler, and Archdeacon William Paley. Paley claimed that the best argument for a benevolent God was the beneficent design that we see in nature.

Out of the work of these Anglican divines came a new kind of Christianity. We may call it Enlightenment Christianity and note that it had four main points.

1. We are reasonable and free creatures, able to fall from goodness and to rise toward goodness. We have a role in our own salvation.
2. Christianity is a simple religion. John Locke reduced its faith to two principles: "Honor Jesus as Lord, and live a good life."
3. The purpose of a Christian is to be good and happy. Ethics is the fulfillment of religion. The preacher, therefore, will see first of all to the moral instruction of his congregation. He will not trust the sacraments of the church (neither baptism nor communion) to convey an automatic sanctity to his people, unless they themselves are morally regenerate. The preacher will urge them more to improve themselves than to enjoy themselves, because if they improve themselves they will inevitably be happy.
4. The conversion to God is a lifelong experience of discipline and trial, not a single flash of emotional transformation. One may experience a sudden conversion, powerful and emotional, but that in itself proves nothing. One's ultimate test before God is the lifelong experience of trial and discipline through which one overcomes bondage to sin.

These four principles of Enlightenment Christianity, an intellectual import from England and Scotland, blended well with the Puritan assumptions in New England. Here was a country whose population had increased almost tenfold between 1713 and 1776 (from 360 thousand to over three million). Here was a country fervently capitalistic and individualistic, a country that prized hard work and frugality, whose people believed that their labor would be richly rewarded, especially in the prosperous seaboard cities. Here was a people moving toward self-sufficiency, toward middle-class democracy, white and male to be sure, but still an improvement over the feudal culture of European nations.

Stir this sense of economic, social, and political optimism together with the Puritan sense of responsibility and its faith in congregational government; combine the resulting mixture with the philosophical and theological elements of Enlightenment Christianity, shake, bake, and set for fifty years, and you have the makings of the American intellectual pie in which regional differences were dissolved in an intellectual consensus that included most of America's leaders—Ethan Allen, Benjamin Franklin, John Adams, George Washington, James Madison, and Thomas Jefferson.

It is for this reason, I believe, that Sydney Ahlstrom says in his great work, *A Religious History of the American People*, "The liberal 'revolution' at King's Chapel between 1776 and 1778 was outwardly an isolated phenomenon. Yet it was symptomatic of spiritual changes in the Boston conscience that ran far deeper than men realized, and it proved a portent of other disruptions soon to follow."[2]

This was the tradition in which James Freeman was schooled by his family, church, school, and college. At Harvard, in addition to studying Latin, Greek, logic, and natural philosophy, he probably read Locke, Doddridge, Whitby, John Taylor's *Scriptural Doctrine of Original Sin*, Thomas Emlyn's *An Humble Inquiry into the Scripture Account of Jesus Christ*, and Samuel Clarke's Boyle lectures on the being and attributes of God, as well as possibly more orthodox writers such as Richard Baxter and Isaac Watts. By Freeman's time, students at Harvard were writing their senior theses on such subjects as the freedom of the will, the nature of virtue, the function of conscience, and the proper relationship between religion and ethics.

Harvard was becoming more liberal. Freeman's own minister, Charles Chauncy, was a leading overseer. Students were reading the works of Isaac Newton and John Locke and writing essays on the function of conscience and the freedom of the will. Professor Wigglesworth lectured on comparative religions. Library hours were expanded, and young ladies were allowed to attend student theatricals.

After graduating from the college, Freeman read recommended theological books and discussed them with a minister in the vicinity of Cambridge for one year. It would be interesting to know with whom he studied and whether he was in Concord when the college resided there for a year.

During this time Freeman wrote to his friend, Edward Bangs, "How do you proceed in law, Ned? I suppose you make your ground good as you go along. No slipping of your foot through some weak part, and beginning your study anew. Would to God that could be my fate. But in my science there are many such weak places, and I am obliged to walk as lightly as a lover to the bed of his mistress thro' the chamber of an old jealous father, lest I should break a hole in it, tumble in, and draw the whole of it after in ruin and confusion."[3]

Most candidates for ministry read for three years, but a war was going on and after a year Freeman went to the family homestead in Barnstable and drilled Continental troops on the town green. By 1780 his mother had died and his father moved the family business to Quebec. In the summer of 1780 Freeman took his sister and younger brothers to join their father in Quebec. His ship, fitted out as cartel, supposedly had permission to operate in both British and American waters; but the governor of Quebec refused to recognize its neutral status and placed James Freeman on board a guard ship. By December he was allowed to go ashore on parole, and there he remained until the summer of 1782 when the governor allowed him to return to New York.

The ship that was to take him to New York was captured within a week by a privateer from Salem and Freeman was taken to that town. In August he came to Boston and then visited his family in Barnstable and friends in Walpole.

At this time King's Chapel was without a minister and almost without a congregation. Many Patriot families had left, never to return, when the siege of Boston began in April 1775. All Loyalist families left with the British troops on March 15, 1776. The Old South congregation worshiped in King's Chapel for five years, but in the fall of 1782 decided to return to their own restored meetinghouse by February of the next year. Joseph May, a member of King's Chapel, recalled some forty years later that not more than a dozen families belonged to King's Chapel at that time. The Senior Warden, Dr. Thomas Bulfinch, decided to find a minister who might then find a congregation.

According to William Bentley, who recorded this in his diary twenty years later, Bulfinch, upon the advice of his brother-in-law, Dr. Samuel Cooper of the Brattle Street Church, tried to interest Bentley himself in the King's Chapel pulpit. When Bentley declined, Bulfinch, against Cooper's advice, sought out Nathaniel Fisher who turned him down and eventually went to the Episcopal church in Salem.

According to Bentley,

To supply this Church, which as a building & a congregation would bear comparison with any in America, was an object of too great importance to be forgotten, especially in the time of a revolution. The English Church were [sic] very nearly attached to the cause of the parent Country, & were [sic] regarded with that peculiar jealousy which the desertion of the greater part of its ministers had inspired, so that its members dared not to employ its open interference in the first steps to supply this Church. Dr. Cooper who had seen the influence of this Church under royal patronage, discovered an opportunity to sever it from the Communion, which would have urged the same temper, if not with the same success. He prevailed on his brother [Thomas Bulfinch, actually, as we have said, his brother-in-law], who took the direction of its affairs, to provide a dissenter, or a more moderate clergyman, who would be interested in retaining the good will of the Congregational churches."[4]

This is the only comment that we have to this effect, and it is hard to ascertain its accuracy, since it was written twenty years later.

Bulfinch, now twice frustrated, must have heard about James Freeman through the latter's classmate George Minot, a member of King's Chapel. After going to Cambridge and failing to find him there, Bulfinch wrote to Freeman in Walpole on September 8, 1782, and asked him if he would come to Boston and discuss the possibility of filling the pulpit of the Chapel. Freeman replied that he would be in Boston on September 20, saying that he would be "throwing himself upon the candour of gentlemen for whose character and abilities I entertain the highest veneration and exposing myself in a town where I shall tremble under the eye of the most accurate judges."[5] He promised to hold himself disengaged until he heard from them, this despite an offer from a church in Providence.

The interview must have gone well. On September 26 Bulfinch sent to Freeman, still in Boston, a formal letter requesting that he come to the Chapel in the capacity of a reader for six months. He was to read the service twice each Sunday and on saint's days. He was to deliver a sermon of his own when convenient and read such other sermons as he thought best. Bulfinch added "The Proprietors consent to such alterations in the service as are made by the Rev. Mr. Parker and leave the use of the Creed of St. Athanasius at your discretion."[6] Parker at Trinity Church, then at the corner of Bishop's Alley and Hawley Street (the present site of Filene's department store) did not read prayers for the King, the Royal Family, or Parliament.

Freeman responded on the same day that Bulfinch's letter was written: "I trust that the Proprietors of the Chapel will view with candour the exertions of a very young man and pardon the imperfections of a person who will always esteem himself peculiarly happy if he has an opportunity to add either to their pleasure or their welfare."[7] He advised his father not to address his letters with the title "Reverend" since he was not ordained. "The situation is novel," he explained.

That Bulfinch should allow an inexperienced, young lay reader to decide when and where the Athanasian Creed was to be used tells us something about the few remaining members of King's Chapel. They were *moderates* in theology, not radicals, not even liberals, but broad-minded Anglicans who felt that they were called more to imitate Christ than to venerate him. George Minot, Freeman's friend with whom he lived on Spring Street (until he married Martha Curtis Clarke in 1788), wrote in his diary, "I verily think that my salvation does not depend upon my believing the Trinity or the unity of the Godhead, nor am I a better christian . . . [if I] support . . . [Christ's] equality with the Father or for asserting the omnipotence of the Father over the Son, than if I sincerely imitate the example of one and reverentially adore the other."[8] Notice that Minot chooses neither Unitarianism or Trinitarianism. He asserts the importance of works over belief.

Minot was typical of the people attracted to the Chapel by James Freeman's preaching. They were young entrepreneurs, ready to make money, buy homes, raise families, and use their gain to build a city and culture that they hoped, would outshine the brightest urban gems in Europe. These young Boston merchants were optimistic and energetic, and they were looking for a preacher to articulate their loyalties and goals, to sympathize with them in their struggles, and to represent to them the best they hoped to be. Such a man they found in Freeman.

On October 18, 1782, Freeman delivered his inaugural sermon and later described the occasion to his sister. "The first time I preached at the Chapel, Boston, the church was open with some degree of splendour. There was an anthem and other pieces of music exceedingly beautiful. The audience was immense, and of such a kind as to overpower all confidence. I felt the weight of it most sensibly. . . . The exertions I am, obliged to make on such occasions keep my mind in a continual agitation. There is a pain attending it, but there is also a pleasure."[9]

On October 20 the Proprietors voted to pay him £12 per

month. By December, Christopher Minot wrote to Timothy Dwight, "James Freeman gains applause every day, and makes a capital preacher, I assure you. He'll be settled at the Chapel as soon as Congress appoints out some way for his Ordination, as well as any other Church Priest without going to Old England for orders."[10]

Freeman himself was not unhappy despite his "agitation." He wrote to his father, "I am now confirmed in my opinion that I shall obtain settlement for life. The church increases every day, and I am happy to find that my friends are still very partial. I trust, you believe, that by entering into this line, I have imbibed no high church notions. . . . The proprietors of the Chapel are very liberal in their notions. They allow me to make several alterations in the service, which liberty I frequently use."[11]

Freeman then reports to his father that the church has already grown in only three months from forty to eighty families, and that his salary will be raised to £250 per annum if all proves well at the end of the trial. He concludes, "If at any time of life I knew what contentment was, it is at the present. I enjoy a tranquillity of mind which makes every object around me pleasing."[12]

The changes that Freeman first introduced were modest. He dropped the Creed from the Eucharist and the prayers for royalty. He emended parts of the Litany. And for a time he was happy with all that happened in his growing, happy church. He describes a current plan for organizing an American Anglican church without bishops. "Perhaps," he tells his father, "I may be the first minister ordained in America upon this new establishment."[13] That, of course, was not to be.

The year 1783 was a quiet one for the congregation and minister. In February the Old South congregation returned to their meetinghouse. On April 21 the Proprietors chose Freeman to be their minister with a salary of £200 per annum. Freeman wrote his father: "The proprietors of that church invited me to settle. I accepted their invitation and am now fixed for life. The salary . . . will probably be enlarged as the church grows. But if it does not, I am easy. I never expected to enjoy half that sum . . . [and] never was so happy in my life."[14]

At that time, no one knew that ten of the fourteen Episcopal clergy in Connecticut had met secretly in Woodbury on March 25 to choose one of their number to seek consecration as the first American Episcopal bishop. The man whom they elected was a brilliant, energetic, and at times irascible priest named Samuel Seabury. Little did the enlightened Christians at King's Chapel know how much this man would mean to them.

Freeman's letter to his father on August 2, 1783 tells us what was on his mind.

I am settled but not ordained; consequently am only a lay preacher. It has been usual in some small episcopal churches in this state where people have not been able to procure or maintain a clergyman, to hire a person to read some parts of the liturgy and a printed sermon to them. I was invited at first by the proprietors of the Chapel in that capacity, and all good high churchmen supposed, that I should conduct myself as all other lay readers do, and not presume to usurpt upon any of the prerogatives of a priest.

But this is an age, and America the country, of innovations. Instead of being confined to the desk, to read merely, I have been obliged by my parishioners to exercise all the functions of a clergyman, except that of reading the absolution, administering the two ordinances, and marrying. In order that I should be enabled to perform these, it is necessary that I should obtain orders. Many plans for this purpose have been proposed, but none yet settled. To go to England for them would be pleasant enough, but base and servile for a free republican. . . . Some have proposed to found bishoprics in America but such a plan is very unpopular. For my own part, I could wish that Presbyterian ordination might be adopted. The bishops, in my opinion, are useless and in this country would be a pernicious order.

I like the liturgy of the church of England but am fond

of the independent form of ecclesiastical government.
The New England churches are upon the best establishment in the world. . . . I am endeavoring, in private, to
bring the proprietors of the chapel to this opinion; and
meet with some success. . . . It is now Saturday night and
my sermon for tomorrow is not ready.[15]

Freeman's bliss did not last beyond 1783. As time passed he
became more and more uncomfortable with the 1662 liturgy
despite the emendations permitted to him. How could a young
man raised at First Church, the Latin School, and Harvard
College, and imbued with the spirit of American egalitarian-
ism be content with a prayerbook written by Trinitarian tradi-
tionalists?

Freeman, by then, was theologically 1) an Arminian who
believed that human beings, born with freedom and reason,
were, in large part responsible for their salvation; 2) an Arian
who believed that Jesus Christ was a semi-angelic being, a
savior, but not God himself; and 3) an egalitarian who could
not believe that priests had the power to absolve people of
their sins nor that sacraments were effective by themselves.

Freeman *later* became a Socinian, that is, one who believed
that Jesus was a man, but one made perfect by God and
appointed to reveal God's will. In 1788 he wrote to his colleague Theophilus Lindsey, "I find myself daily inclining toward Socinianism. I cannot resist the force of Dr. Priestley's
reasoning, nor, upon the supposition of the pre-existence of
Christ, rationally interpret those texts which style him a man.
. . . Should I ever become a simple unitarian, I shall be as ready
to declare it, as I lately was to declare that I was an Arian."[16]
Later that year he wrote to Lindsey, thanking him for a book,
"I trust that it will be the means of removing from the minds
of many free inquirers some prejudice which they entertain
against the doctrine of the simple humanity of Christ. The
Socinian scheme is already less frightful among us than it was a
few years ago, and it begins to have some publick advocates."[17]

Freeman did not yet believe in universal salvation, even
though his former pastor, Charles Chauncy, had at last pub-

lished his work on this subject. In 1782 he wrote his father, "I find that the doctrine of universal salvation has spread with a great rapidity. The women, in particular, are very fond of it. It suits the benevolence of their temper so well, that it is no wonder that they admit it. In saying this I do not mean that I myself believe it."[18] Finding Dr. Chauncy's arguments not "perfectly satisfying," Freeman adds, "In determining that all men shall finally be saved we seem, to enter too deeply into the counsels of the Deity. In speaking of the future state of mankind the Divine Being has thought fit to deliver himself with some degree of obscurity."[19]

Later Freeman wrote to his father, "The controversy concerning the doctrine of universal salvation has almost entirely subsided. The friends of Mr. Murray, the gentleman who believes that there will be no kind of future punishment, propose to build a church in this town which shall be open to all sects, from Roman Catholics down to Quakers. The plan, I think, is too romantically liberal ever to take place."[20] A few months after Freeman wrote this letter, John Murray established the First Universalist Society of Boston.

Freeman was reluctant to embrace Universalism, possibly, because like most Unitarian ministers he believed passionately in free will and could not stomach a universalism that predestined everyone to redemption. We have no record of Freeman exchanging or conversing with the Rev. Hosea Ballou whose Second Universalist Church stood for many years across School Street from King's Chapel.

Let us leave Freeman for a moment and look again across the Atlantic to another series of events that would make a mighty difference to the Stone Chapel. (In deference to Republican sentiment, the title "King's Chapel" was changed to Stone Chapel after the Revolution.)

In 1773, the same year that James Freeman entered Harvard College, an Anglican priest named Theophilus Lindsey was defrocked and dispossessed of his parish in the village of Catterick. Lindsey resolved to go to London and found an independent Anglican church with a reformed (or "enlightened?") prayerbook. On his way to London, Lindsey stopped at the home of his friend and colleague, John Disney, in Swinderly in Lincolnshire. Disney showed Lindsey a copy that he had made of Samuel Clarke's reformed Anglican prayerbook. (Samuel Clarke, rector of St. James, Piccadilly, had secretly edited a copy of the 1662 prayerbook, eliminating most Trinitarian prayers and litanies.) Lindsey realized that Clarke's non-Trinitarian prayerbook was the very model that he needed for creating his own prayerbook, and so he followed it, although he made far more radical changes than did Clarke.

Lindsey established a new congregation on Essex Street in London with its own prayerbook. They held their first worship service on April 17, 1774, and Benjamin Franklin, the American enlightened Christian par excellence, was present.

In 1783 a member of Lindsey's congregation, the Reverend William Hazlitt, sailed for America hoping to find a pulpit here. He preached in the Philadelphia area for some time, attracting much attention but no settlement. When he heard that the Brattle Street Church in Boston was open, he came to Boston, arriving on May 15, 1784.

Armed with a letter of introduction from a Philadelphia minister, he went on that very day to the home of Dr. Charles Chauncy where he found (of all things) the Boston association of ministers at their monthly meeting. The subject of their conversation was ordination and before the meeting closed Hazlitt was asked his opinion. Hazlitt, never at a loss for words, declared that the scripture permitted the lay members of a church to ordain someone to the ministry without any clergy present, that is, quite literally, without benefit of clergy.

According to one source "Mr. Freeman upon hearing this jumped from his seat in a kind of transport, saying 'I wish you could prove that, Sir.' The gentleman answered that 'few things would admit of an easier proof,' and from that moment a thorough intimacy commenced between him and Mr. F."[21]

We must assume it was from Hazlitt that James Freeman, himself unschooled in liturgy, learned of Samuel Clarke's and Theophilus Lindsey's revisions of the Anglican prayerbook and found in them the models upon which he would soon revise King's Chapel's liturgy. It must have been Hazlitt who convinced Freeman that lay members of his congregation could ordain him to the ministry without the authority of either a bishop or council of ministers. Hazlitt's son, the famous essayist, wrote some years later, "It was while we resided at Weymouth that my father assisted in preparing a liturgy for his [Freeman's] church which had been episcopal and furnished him with a form of prayer used by Mr. Lindsey in Essex Street Chapel, which they adapted to suit the Transatlantic Church."[22]

Freeman himself wrote, "Before Mr. Hazlitt came to Boston, the Trinitarian doxology was almost universally used. That honest good man prevailed upon several respectable ministers to omit it. Since his departure, the number of those who repeat only scriptural doxologies has greatly increased."[23]

Freeman's praise for Hazlitt is curious when compared with the judgment of other clergy. Jeremy Belknap found his company "disgusting," and John Eliot called him "the most conceited man I ever met with." Two years later William Bentley wrote of Hazlitt, "While at Boston he attached himself to the ingenuous Mr. Freeman now Reader at King's chapel and led that worthy man to some hasty measures in revising the Liturgy which may prove fatal to his establishment in that Society."[24] Bentley may have seen his friend's undue susceptibility to influence, but we must add that without Hazlitt, James Freeman and King's Chapel might never have found models for liturgical reform and independent ordination.

Freeman found the doctrine of the Trinity especially troubling. Francis Greenwood, his friend, colleague, and successor, later wrote "He communicated his difficulties to those of his friends with whom he was most intimate. He would come into their houses and say, 'I must leave you. Much as I love you I must leave you. I cannot conscientiously perform the service of the church any longer, as it now stands.' . . . At length . . . it was said, 'why not state your difficulties and the grounds of them publicly to your whole people, that they may be able to judge of the case, and determine whether it is such as to require a separation between you and them, or not?' "[25]

Freeman preached the first of such sermons on November 14, 1784. Greenwood tells us, ". . . he plainly stated his dissatisfaction with the trinitarian portions of the Liturgy, went fully into an examination of the trinitarian doctrine, and gave his reasons for rejecting it. He has himself assured me that when he delivered those sermons, he was under a strong impression that they would be the last he should ever pronounce from this pulpit. . . . [But] He was heard patiently, kindly, attentively. The greater part of his hearers responded to his sentiments, and resolved to alter their Liturgy, and retain their pastor."[26]

Strangely, on that same day that James Freeman preached this sermon, Samuel Seabury was being ordained to the episcopate by three dissident Scottish bishops in Aberdeen. Having arrived in London on July 7, 1783, he tried unsuccessfully for over a year to convince the English bishops to ordain him, and finally went northward to Scotland where he found sympathy among the dissident Anglicans (a century-old remnant of those who were still loyal to the line of James II). Of course, no *quid* comes without its *quo*, and after the ceremony Seabury agreed to introduce the Scottish communion rite into the new American Episcopal prayerbook and to oppose the lay election of bishops in the American church.

Before King's Chapel could proceed with emending its prayerbook, the Proprietors had to be sure who owned the pews of the church. (The owners, or proprietors, of the pews legally owned the building and constituted the policy-making body for King's Chapel.) On January 10, 1785, they declared that twenty-nine pews had been forfeited by their absentee owners, and they offered to pay £16 for every vacated pew to the former owner if the owner applied within a year from the date of their vote. They then offered these twenty-nine pews for sale together with the Governor's pew and eight others. We may assume that these pews were bought by new, liberal parishioners who had been attracted to the Chapel by Freeman's preaching.

On February 20 the Proprietors voted "That it is the sense of the Proprietors of this Church that it is essentially necessary that there be some alterations made in some parts of the Liturgy now used in the church, That a committee be appointed to report such alterations as they shall judge necessary, That the committee consist of seven in addition to the wardens, and that they consult and communicate with the Rev. Mr. Freeman upon the subject of this, [and] That the same committee report whether any means of ordination can be obtained."[27]

The wardens were Thomas Bulfinch and Shrimpton Hutchinson. The other committee members were Samuel Breck, John Gardiner, John Haskins, Charles Miller, Perez Morton, John Wheelwright, and Charles Williams. It was a committee of established members; the first five were Old (pre-1782) Proprietors.

The committee reported to the annual meeting of the Proprietors always held on the Monday after Easter, as follows, "That some alterations are essentially necessary to be made in the liturgy. The several alterations were then read and considered and debated at several adjournments, each paragraph being distinctly considered and a vote taken thereon."[28]

We must realize that the members of King's Chapel, although sympathetic to their minister's desires, were not ready to amend their liturgy as thoroughly as he wished. In some places they followed Lindsey's lead. For example, they consented to the scriptural doxology in place of the trinitarian doxology (which begins "Glory be to the Father, and to the Son, and to the Holy Ghost"). They consented to the minister's prayer for absolution in place of the priest's pronouncement of absolution. They were willing to see the litany revised as well as the service of Holy Communion.

But in many matters the laity followed their own mind rather than Lindsey's (or Freeman's). They preferred to continue to pray "through Jesus Christ our Lord." They revised the Te Deum rather than reject it. They preferred Saint Paul's benediction ("And now may the grace of our Lord Jesus Christ, etc.") to an Old Testament benediction that Lindsey used. They kept the Venite that Lindsey had replaced with Psalm 50, and their editing of the Litany and eucharist was far more conservative than Lindsey's.

A thorough comparison of the Clarke, Lindsey, and King's Chapel liturgies may yield more telling information, but it seems safe to say that King's Chapel was closer to Clarke than Lindsey. A year after this endeavor Freeman wrote to Lindsey, "I wish the work was more worthy of your approbation. I can only say that I endeavored to make it so by attempting to introduce your liturgy entire. But the people of the church were not ready for so great a change. Some defects and improprieties I was under the necessity of retaining, for the sake of inducing them to omit the most objectionable parts of the old service, the Athanasian prayers. Perhaps in some future day when their minds become more enlightened, they may consent to a further alteration."[29]

What James Freeman hoped for may perhaps be best seen in the second edition of the prayerbook, which appeared in 1811. In April of 1805 James Freeman, Ebenezer Oliver, and Joseph May proposed alterations to the Vestry; and on March 19, 1806, the Vestry voted that "Each Family be furnished with a copy of the Morning Prayer as lately amended and be requested to examine the same, so far as to decide the question of adopting it, instead of the present form, and at a special meeting of the proprietors and congregation to be held for that purpose on Sunday, March 20 current."[30] We have no record of such a meeting being held.

In 1807 a new committee was asked to prepare a new edition of the liturgy and report as soon as possible to the Vestry and congregation. Again, nothing happened, and in 1808 the Vestry, evidently needing more copies of the prayerbook, voted to print over 250 copies of the 1785 edition. It was not until after the ordination of Samuel Cary on September 1, 1809, that action began.

Although Cary was new to the church, the Vestry on May 1, 1810, appointed him to the committee formed in 1807 and requested that the Committee "attend to the business as soon as may be." By January 1811 Cary reported to the Vestry that he had finished revising the psalms and received permission to revise the services. By February the Committee completed their recommendations, which the Vestry accepted and incorporated into the second edition of the prayerbook, published that same year.

The Committee dropped the Apostle's Creed from Morning Prayer and the prayer for protection against "all false doctrines, heresies, and schism" in the Litany. The committee added four complete Sunday services taken from the prayerbooks of liberal churches in Liverpool and Salisbury in England, probably intending that these services would be used at times in place of Morning and Evening Prayer. This did not happen.

In his preface to the fifth edition (printed in 1841) Francis Greenwood wrote, "One of the three Additional Services has been omitted. The other two are retained, not because they are used, but because at some times they may be found useful." These 1811 services were dropped in the 1918 edition because the congregation, as the preface put it, "having tasted the new wine, decided that they liked the old better."

Let us return now to the publication of the first prayerbook. In May of 1785, possibly after a six-week trial of the proposed material, there was sufficient consensus in the church for the wardens to order the paper for the new prayerbook at a cost of £66. On June 19 the Proprietors met and voted on the question: "That, the Common Prayer as it now stands amended be adopted by this Church as the form of Prayer, to be used, in future by this Church and Congregation."

The Yeas were Thomas Bulfinch, Andrew Johonnot, Charles Miller, Robert Hewes, Thomas Clement, Joseph Earyes, Mary Johonnot (by her son and proxy), Henry Johnson, John Gardiner, John Wheelwright, Joseph May, John Jutan, Ebenezer Oliver, George R. Minot, John Amory, John Templeman, Joseph Barrell, Joseph Coolidge, Jacob Porter, Samuel Breck, and Perez Morton—twenty-one in all, the first seven being Old Proprietors.

The Nays were James Ivers, Barlow Trecothick (in London) by proxy, Charles Williams, John Haskins, Ambrose Vincent, Theodore Dehon, Matthew Nasro, and John Box—all eight being Old Proprietors.

According to the testimony of Joseph May given forty years later,[31] the last three were members of Trinity Church, which they had joined in 1776, and where they had worshiped since. John Haskins, James Ivers, and Charles Williams left the church. Ambrose Vincent continued as a member and served in the Vestry in 1786 and 1787.

On the day after the Proprietors had so voted, Samuel Seabury landed in Newport, ready to assume his episcopal duties. King's Chapel's actions did not go unnoticed. Early in May, Samuel Parker, rector of Trinity, wrote to a friend in England, "Your old friend Troutbeck's congregation [King's Chapel], . . . a lay reader at their head, have altered the liturgy according to the Arian Scheme upon the Plan of Lindsay."[32]

Joel Barlow, the poet laureate of Connecticut Congregationalism and the contributor of eight doxologies printed at the back of the new prayerbook, wrote from Hartford to Perez Morton, "The liberality and sublimity of the plan will recommend it to the candid and benevolent of all denominations of Christians, it cannot be objected to by any order of rational beings."[33]

A copy sent to Nathaniel Fisher, the Episcopal rector in Salem, was returned without comment. William White, the Philadelphia rector and soon-to-be bishop, responded more considerately to Charles Miller who sent him a copy. He praised the book on two points, but added, "I think your congregation will find it difficult to justify these two things: First, their leaving out every invocation of the Redeemer; and secondly, the making of the alterations of the liturgy a congregational act."[34] He expressed his fear that King's Chapel had become Arian or Socinian, and he questioned the congregation's right to hold the title to the building, if they had left the faith of their forbears. White sent this letter through Samuel Parker at Trinity, asking Parker to read it before passing it on.

Freeman wrote his father in July, "nothing material has happened except that the reformed Prayer book at the end of the limited time was voted in by a large majority. This glorious success makes me very happy. I send you the remaining pages."[35] There ensued a long correspondence in which Constant Freeman questioned the exclusion of prayers addressed to Christ and his son defended them on the grounds of "inclusiveness." Freeman may have been a little hurt by his father's criticisms for in December he says, "My aversion to religious controversy prevents my enlarging at this time. I will only repeat an observation which I have already made, that the new Liturgy is calculated not for one particular sect, but for all Christians, whatsoever their particular tenets may be."[36]

It is often the fate of those who hope to be most inclusive to find themselves as particular a group as any other, and this, of course, King's Chapel eventually discovered. In looking back on this time, Freeman said, forty years later, "The alterations made in the Book of Common Prayer were not intended by ourselves, in whatever light they might be viewed by others, as a public manifestation of dissent and secession from the Church of England or any other church. The Church of England had expired among the flames of the revolution; but we expected, or at least hoped that a new and more beautiful Church would arise from its ashes—an American Protestant Episcopal Church which should be purified from all the puerilities, superstitions and corruptions of the old establishment. We wished to become a part of this Church, or even of one which was less pure, provided we might be allowed to omit those parts of the Liturgy which we could not conscientiously read."[37]

This of course could not be. Freeman and his parish had already begun their Exodus, heading for a place neither promised nor known. In the summer of 1785 they placed an order with Peter Edes for printing six hundred copies of a small octavo edition of four hundred and twenty-two pages. Edes' bill was £97. For another £37 William Green gathered (bound) two hundred copies. On September 23, 1785, according to William Bentley, the "reformed liturgy" as he called it, was read in Boston for the first time. The storm was yet to come.

Notes

1. Philip Marson, *Breeder of Democracy* (Cambridge: Schenkman, 1970), p.v. Quoted in E. Digby Baltzell, *Puritan Boston and Quaker Philadelphia* (New York: The Free Press, 1979), p. 270.

2. Sydney E. Ahlstrom, *A Religious History of the American People* (New Haven: Yale University Press, 1972), p. 389.

3. James Freeman to Edward Bangs, July 17, 1778, Collection of Massachusetts Historical Society (hereafter referred to as MHS).

4. William Bentley, *The Diary of William Bentley* (Gloucester, MA: Peter Smith, 1962), Vol. 2, entry for March 7, 1802.

5. James Freeman to Thomas Bulfinch, September 10, 1782, MHS.

6. Thomas Bulfinch to James Freeman, September 26, 1782, MHS.

7. James Freeman to the Wardens of King's Chapel, September 26, 1782, Collection at Houghton Library (hereafter referred to as HL), Harvard University, Cambridge, MA.

8. George Richards Minot, *Diary*, Collection of the MHS, First Series Vol. 8:98-105, entry for December 24, 1782.

9. James Freeman to Lois Freeman, December 24, 1782, in *Minot Family Letters*, p.10.

10. Christopher Minot to Timothy Dwight, December 14, 1782, Sedgewick Collection, Box 1-10, MHS.

11. James Freeman to Constant Freeman, quoted in Henry Wilder Foote, "James Freeman and King's Chapel," *The Religious Magazine and Monthly Review*, June 1873, 49(6): 509.

12. *Ibid.*

13. *Ibid.*

14. James Freeman to Constant Freeman, May 12, 1783, HL.

15. James Freeman to Constant Freeman, August 2, 1783, HL.

16. James Freeman to Theophilus Lindsey, March 29, 1788, Collection of Doctor Williams's Library, (hereafter referred to as DWL). 10 Gordon Square, London.

17. James Freeman to Theophilus Lindsey, October 15, 1788, DWL.

18. James Freeman to Constant Freeman, December 24, 1782, HL.

19. *Ibid.*

20. James Freeman to Constant Freeman, March 10, 1784, HL.

21. Foote, "James Freeman and King's Chapel," pp. 512-513.

22. William Hazlitt, *Four Generations of a Literary Family, Volume 1.* (London: George Redway, 1897), p. 44.

23. James Freeman to Theophilus Lindsey, June 1789, quoted in Thomas Belsham, *Memoirs of the Late Reverend Theophilus Lindsey*, (London: J. Johnson and Co., 1812), p. 240.

24. Bentley, *Diary*, Vol. 1, entry for April 9, 1786.

25. Francis William Pitt Greenwood, "A Sermon Preached in King's Chapel, November 22, 1835, the Sunday after the Funeral of the Reverend James Freeman, D.D." (Boston: Russell, Shattuck and Williams, 1835), p. 9.

26. *Ibid.*, p. 10.
27. Record of the Proprietors of Pews of King's Chapel, February 20, 1785, MHS.
28. *Ibid.*, March 27, 1785, MHS.
29. James Freeman to Theophilus Lindsey, July 7, 1786, quoted in Belsham, p. 238.
30. Records of the Wardens and Vestry of King's Chapel, March 19, 1806, MHS.
31. "The Deposition of Joseph May," in *Annals of King's Chapel*, Vol. 3, ed. John Carroll Perkins (Boston: Little Brown, 1940), pp. 358-359.
32. Samuel Parker to Samuel Peters, May 7, 1785, in *Seabury Traditions, The Reconstructed Journal of Connecticut's Diocesan*, Vol. 2, ed. Kenneth Walter Cameron (Hartford: Transcendental Books, 1983), p. 6.
33. Joel Barlow to Perez Morton, June 18, 1785, Archives of King's Chapel at the Parish House.
34. William White to Charles Miller, December 1, 1785, quoted in Marion Hatchett, "The Making of the First American Prayerbook," submitted in partial fulfillment of the requirements for the degree of Doctor of Theology in the General Theological Seminary, New York City, February 1, 1972, p. 350.
35. James Freeman to Constant Freeman, July 15, 1785, HL.
36. James Freeman to Constant Freeman, December 21, 1785, HL.
37. Foote, "James Freeman and King's Chapel," p. 8.

THREE

Without Benefit of Clergy

*An account of King's Chapel's attempt to secure episcopal
ordination for James Freeman and their eventual decision to
independently ordain him to the ministry of this church.*

————————————

While James Freeman and the Proprietors of King's Chapel
were revising the church liturgy, the clergy of the other Anglican churches were organizing an American Protestant Episcopal church. On September 27, 1785, only four days after the
first public reading of the reformed liturgy in King's Chapel,
a convention was held in Philadelphia attended by sixteen
clerical and twenty-four lay delegates from the Episcopal
churches in the so-called "southern states," namely, New York,
New Jersey, Pennsylvania, Maryland, Delaware, Virginia, and
South Carolina. (The "northern states" were the New England states.)

Connecticut refused to send delegates to this convention,
which had invited their bishop, Samuel Seabury, the only
bishop in America at the time, not in his capacity as bishop but
as a parish priest. This was a slight that the Connecticut
Episcopalians could not ignore. Furthermore, they suspected
that the southern states wished to make clergy and laity equal
in the new church, and these men who had gone through such
efforts to elevate one of their number to a bishopric were not
going to help any such effort. The clergy from the other New
England states also did not attend this convention. Although
not as high church as their Connecticut neighbors, they were

wary of what might come from it.

The convention of southern states began its work by voting to ask the English bishops to consecrate Samuel Provoost, the Loyalist rector of Trinity Church in New York City, and William White, the rector of the Philadelphia church, as the first bishops in the soon-to-be-formed American Episcopal church. Obviously, the convention did not yet recognize Samuel Seabury as a real bishop because he had been consecrated by Scottish bishops who themselves were not recognized by the English bishops.

The convention also appointed a committee to revise the 1662 prayerbook for use in America. When this committee reported back to the convention on October 5, the delegates agreed to delete the Athanasian and Nicene creeds, to expurgate the imprecatory parts of the psalms and to reword and rearrange the prayers. The initial agreement on these radical changes indicate that many American Episcopalians shared James Freeman's impatience with a liturgy that they had inherited from England. The convention then appointed a committee chaired by William White and charged it to publish the new liturgy as soon as possible. This new liturgy was published on April 1, 1786. The convention took all these actions without the presence or concurrence of the northern (New England) states.

We must understand that the northern and southern states had for some years mistrusted each other, and this mistrust might have prevented the creation of a single Episcopal church in America. This division was exacerbated by the enmity between Samuel Seabury and Samuel Provoost, who habitually misrepresented the name of his adversary as "Dr. Cobra." Clearly, Provoost felt the greater animus, yet Seabury himself did little to relieve the apprehensions of the low clergy to the south.

The southern states met for a second time in September 1786 after hearing from the English bishops. The English bishops were clearly unhappy about such actions as removing both the Athanasian and the Nicene creeds, and they warned their American brothers against violating Anglican tradition.

They suggested that the ordination of Messrs. Provoost and White would depend upon the kind of liturgy that the Americans decided to follow.

The southern delegates, in renewing their request for consecration, assured the English bishops that they had made no alterations or omissions in the *Book of Common Prayer* "except those needed to make it consistent with our civil constitutions or such as were calculated to remove objections which it appeared to us more conducive to union and general content to obviate than to dispute. . . . We are now settling and ordering the affairs of our Church," they concluded, "And if wisely done, we shall have reason to promise ourselves all the advantages that can result from stability and union."[1] More persuasive than their assurances was the fact that the proposed 1785 prayerbook was never officially adopted. Not until 1789 did the American Episcopal churches, both southern and northern states, adopt a liturgy.

During this time King's Chapel was seeking ordination for their lay reader. James Freeman, aware of how radical the new prayerbook might seem to other Anglicans, defended it to William White. He explained that King's Chapel had not revised its liturgy "until the opinion of the Episcopal Churches in the New York Convention was known. But when we found that a reformation was not likely to take place with respect to the great object of religious worship, we concluded that we had a right to make the correction of the Service a congregational act."[2]

Freeman knew that the convention of southern churches in New York had agreed that they should "maintain the doctrines of the Gospel, as now held by the Church of England; and shall adhere to the liturgy of the said church, as far as shall be consistent with the American Revolution and the constitutions of the respective states."

"The object of our Society in the new Liturgy," he explained to White, "was to leave out all such expressions as might wound the conscience of the Unitarian, without introducing any which should displease a Trinitarian, . . . [yet] the Society was under no obligation to accommodate themselves to the peculiar speculative principles of a Dr. Priestley or the Socinians."[3]

Referring to the imminent second convention of southern states Freeman warned, "Should the convention . : . not enlarge their plan to this extent, the Congregation worshipping at the Stone Chapel, provided it persevere in its present system, which I have reason to think it will do, must be reduced to the disagreeable necessity of separating itself from the Episcopal church and of availing itself of that resource which the glorious freedom of our country affords, of forming an independent society."[4] Those of course were fighting words.

Samuel Parker, the rector of Trinity Church, scarcely a block from King's Chapel, described that church's predicament to White in a letter dated January of 1786:

> The Committee of that Society who revised their Liturgy, had given out that all the Churches on the Continent to the Southward of Connecticut were in the same Sentiments, and the Liturgy when revised by their Convention then to be held at Philadelphia would be exactly similar to theirs, and they are not a little chagrined to find themselves so much mistaken. . . . I have however no hopes that even your Arguments will convince them of their errors or that they will retract, as long as Mr. Freeman continues as their reader.
>
>   There is but one reason to suspect they ever will, and that is the Difficulty they will find in their present plan of his obtaining Ordination. I have heard that they applied to Dr. Seabury to give him Episcopal Ordination, but that he had refused. And I think by your Ecclesiastical Constitution he must be precluded from obtaining it from any Bishop at the Southward. . . . Should he resource [recourse] to the Congregational Clergy and be ordained by them, all pretence to their being an Episcopal Church must be at an End, and a way will be opened to the minority to recover the house.[5]

Parker saw clearly the dilemma of King's Chapel. They had

already changed the Anglican liturgy at substantial points. If they could not convince Seabury or Provoost to ordain Freeman, they must continue with Freeman as a lay leader, or ordain him themselves. In either case they could not claim to be Episcopal and risked losing their sanctuary to the newly formed Episcopal diocese in a court case.

On February 7, 1786, the Wardens and Vestry of King's Chapel wrote to Seabury, addressing him as "Right Reverend Father" and asking him to ordain Freeman to the priesthood. They said that they hoped

> that you will not consider it an indispensable Condition in this Country that he should be obliged to confess or subscribe to any particular doctrinal system of Faith whatever. And as we are earnestly desirous to preserve the Character of our Episcopal Church, and are determined that Necessity alone shall induce us to adopt any other mode of ordination than is established by that Church, provided it can be done without sacrificing our religious Sentiments, We hope and desire that you will require of the Candidate no other than a general declaration of Faith in the Holy Scriptures, leaving him, and those under his pastoral Care, in Creeds and all doctrinal Questions to God and their Consciences.[6]

When Seabury came to Newport in early March 1786 for an ordination, he found a committee from King's Chapel waiting to discuss their request with him. We have no account of that meeting, and we cannot even be sure that Seabury met with the committee.

We do know that when Seabury came to Boston a week later, he met with James Freeman at the home of Samuel Parker. Of that visit Freeman wrote to his father, "My visit to Bishop Seabury terminated as I expected. Before I waited upon him he gave out that he would never ordain me, but it was necessary to ask the question. He being in Boston last March, a committee of our church waited upon him, and requested him to ordain me, without insisting upon any other conditions than a declaration of faith in the Holy Scriptures."[7]

A week later Seabury wrote Thomas Bulfinch, Senior Warden of King's Chapel, that it was "his desire that they would represent their own case to the Connecticut Clergy, who are to meet, on the Wednesday after Whitsunday, at Stratford." Seabury said that he could represent them himself, "though if one of their own number could take the trouble of so long a journey it would be the more agreeable to him."[8] Seabury explained that he did not intend to evade the opinion of the Massachusetts episcopal clergy, but that he considered the Connecticut clergy to be his advising council, and in this matter wished to consult them. The Bishop added that he hoped to take tea with Dr. Bulfinch and his wife on the coming Thursday.

King's Chapel's cause was not helped by a review of their liturgy that appeared in a London paper on May 13, 1786, and was reprinted in the *Connecticut Journal.* The review listed only major changes which had been made in the 1662 liturgy, but that was enough to infuriate many American clergy. The review noted "The office of Matrimony is shortened, and the word 'obey' is left out in the woman's part."[9]

Nathaniel Fisher, rector of the Episcopal church in Salem and briefly a candidate for King's Chapel's pulpit, wrote to Freeman asking:

> . . . if it is a matter fixed in your mind, to be ordained by the Dissenting Clergy, or the People, why apply to Dr. Seabury—why not receive orders in Town? But you must be best acquainted with your own purposes and prospects. I only have it to lament, among many others of your good Friends, that you cannot enter by the Door, as we Episcopalians stile it. We cannot exchange with you; neither do I see how the dissenting clergy can with propriety. . . . New things generally please for a Season; but I make no doubt that your Society would now, even this day be as well pleased with the old prayer Book, as with their New One. This country is in its Infancy— Boston will do well if they can come up half way to

London. In short, I take it, you run a great risk in your présent plan. . . .[10]

Despite such warnings Freeman kept his appointment with the Episcopal clergy in Connecticut. Although we have no official records of that convention, we have Freeman's account of it in a letter written to his father some months later.

Accordingly, about the beginning of June, I rode to Stratford, where a Convention was holding, carrying with me several letters of recommendation. I waited upon the Bishop's presbyters and delivered my letters. They professed themselves satisfied with the testimonials which they contained of my moral character, &c., but added that they could not recommend me to the Bishop for ordination upon the terms proposed by my church. For a man to subscribe the Scriptures, they said, was nothing, for it could never be determined from that what his creed was. Heretics professed to believe them not less than the orthodox, and made use of them in support of their peculiar opinions. If I could subscribe such a declaration as that I could conscientiously read the whole Book of Common Prayer, they would cheerfully recommend me. I answered that I could not conscientiously subscribe a declaration of that kind. "Why not?" "Because there are some parts of the Book of Common Prayer which I do not approve of." "What parts?" "The prayers to the Son and the Holy Spirit." "You do not then believe the doctrine of the Trinity?" "No." "This appears to us very strange. We can think of no texts which countenance your opinion. We should be glad to hear you mention some."

"It would ill become me, Gentlemen, to dispute with persons of your learning and abilities. But if you will give me leave, I will repeat two passages which appear to me decisive. *There is one God, and one Mediator between God and man, the man Christ Jesus. There is but one God, the*

Father, and one Lord Jesus Christ. [my italics] In both these passages Jesus Christ is plainly distinguished from God, and in the last, that God is expressly declared to be the Father." To this they made no other reply than an ". . . .Ah!" which echoed round the room. "But are they not all attributes of the Father," said one, "attributed to the Son in the Scriptures? not Omnipotence for instance?" "It is true," I answered "that our Saviour says of Himself, *All power is given unto me in Heaven and Earth.* [my italics] You will please to observe here that power is said to be given. It is derived power. It is not self-existent and unoriginated, like that of the Father." "But is not the Son omniscient? Does He not know the hearts of men?" "Yes, He knows them by virtue of the intelligence which He derives from the Father. But, by a like communication, did Peter know the hearts of Ananias and Sapphira."

After some more conversation of the same kind, they told me that it could not possibly be that the Christian world should have been idolators for seventeen hundred years, as they must be according to my opinions. In answer to this, I said that whether they had been idolators or not I would not determine, but that it was full as probable that they would be idolators for seventeen hundred years as they should be Roman Catholics for twelve hundred. They then proceeded to find fault with some parts of the new Liturgy. "We observe that you have converted the absolution to a prayer. Do you mean to deny the power of the Priesthood to absolve the people, and that God has not committed to it the power of remitting sins?" "I meant neither to deny nor to affirm it. The absolution appeared exceptionable to some persons, for which reason it was changed into a prayer, which could be exceptionable to nobody." "But you must be sensible, Mr. Freeman, that Christ instituted an order of Priesthood, and that to them he committed the power of absolving sins. *Whose soever sins ye remit they are remitted unto him, and whose soever sins ye retain they are retained.*" [my italics] To this I made no other reply than a return of their own emphatic Ah! Upon the whole, finding me an incorrigible heretic, they dismissed me without granting my request. They treated me, however, with great candour and politeness, begging me to go home, to read, to alter my opinions, and then to return and receive that Ordination, which they wished to procure me from their Bishop. I left them and proceeded to New York. When there I waited on Mr. Provoost, Rector of the Episcopal Church, who is elected to go to England to be consecrated a Bishop. I found him a liberal man and that he approved of the alterations which had been made at the Chapel. Of him I hope to obtain ordination, *which I am convinced he will cheerfully confer*, [my italics] unless prevented by the bigotry of some of his clergy."[11]

Freeman's journeys were noted by at least two Episcopal clergy. His neighbor, Samuel Parker at Trinity, wrote in September 1786 to William White in Philadelphia:

Mr. Freeman applied to Bishop Seabury in June last for Ordination but at a convention of the Clergy at Stratford the Bishop by Advice of his Clergy did not see fit to confer Order on him upon such a profession of his faith as he thought proper to give which was not more than that he believed the Scriptures. He extended his journey as far as New York and was, as he says, assured by Mr. Provoost that as soon as he should obtain Consecration he would ordain him; this hope alone sustains him at present and was it not for this, I believe he would relinquish all thoughts of subsequently obtaining Orders in the church. Whether Mr. Provoost can do this consistently with the profession he is to make and the Constitution he must submit rests with him.[12]

White replied to Parker in October, stating that he had related this report of Freeman's expectations to Provoost and then added:

Doctor Provoost Authorizes me to declare to you that it is a Falsehood [*sic*], altho' he hopes not of Mr. Freeman's, who may perhaps have been misrepresented to you in this matter. He asks whether he can be thought to have so little Delicacy as to give any promise of this sort even in the most exceptional Case, at a time when he was not even nominated to the Episcopal Character; for it seems the only Conversation he ever held with Mr. Freeman was before his Nomination.

I can myself [continued White to Parker] . . . remember very well Doctor Provoost's mentioning to me in June the last visit of Mr. Freeman; and in giving an account of it, he said, that Mr. Freeman was very candid in the avowal of his Principles, and that he (Doctor Provoost) had told him, it could not be expected he should obtain orders in the Episcopal Church.[13]

Another Episcopal clergy, Ezra Stiles, referred to Freeman as "an adventurous semi-church convert" and to the revised prayerbook as "the new Merchants Liturgy at Boston."[14]

Stiles said of the new liturgy, "The real Divinity and Satisfaction of Christ, and Justification by his Righteousness, with Original Sin, Predestination and Decrees, and the Doctrines of Grace, are all left out of these altered Liturgies in America. In short, they are at best Socinian, and perhaps might be conscientiously used by Deists, who are as ready to honor Jesus as they would Plato or Socrates."[15] In September, Bishop Seabury, without mentioning Freeman or King's Chapel, charged the clergy of his diocese to resist the heresies of Arianism, deism, or Socinianism.

Freeman was of course prepared for a refusal. He wrote to his father:

Should Provoost refuse to ordain me, I shall then endeavor to effect a plan, which I have long had in my head, which is to be ordained by the congregational ministers of this town, or to preach and administer the sacraments without any ordination at all. The last scheme I must approve, for I am fully convinced that he who has devoted his time to the study of divinity, and can find a congregation who are willing to hear him, is to all intents a minister of the gospel; and though the imposition of hands, either through bishops or presbyters, be necessary to constitute him a priest in the eyes of the laws of some countries, yet in the eye of heaven, he has not less of the indelible character than a bishop or patriarch. . . . I am happy that many of my hearers join me in opinion upon this subject.[16]

Two days after Freeman wrote this letter, that is, on November 2, 1786, William White and Samuel Provoost, officially nominated as candidates for the episcopacy by the October convention of southern states, sailed for London. They arrived in twenty-seven days, "one of the fastest trips ever made at that time," according to William Stevens Perry, official historian of the American Protestant Episcopal Church in the last century.

On February 4, 1787, White and Provoost were consecrated by the archbishop of Canterbury in the chapel at Lambeth. One of the chaplains preached on the text, "Let all things be done decently, and in order," from I Corinthians 14:40. On the next day White and Provoost left London for Falmouth and were detained there for a week by poor winds, until they finally left England on February 18. They arrived in New York on the afternoon of Easter Sunday, April 8.

Before he left England, and in fact before his consecration, Samuel Provoost visited his old classmate, John Disney, at Swinburne and according to one source received from him a copy of Samuel Clarke's emendations of the 1662 liturgy. This was the same liturgy that Theophilus Lindsey, another colleague of Disney's, had used as his model in preparing the liturgy of the Essex Street Chapel in London. And it was the liturgy of the Essex Street Chapel that James Freeman had used in preparing the revised liturgy at King's Chapel.

As soon as Freeman read in the *Gazette* of Provoost's return to New York, he wrote him, protesting that he had never claimed that Provoost promised to ordain him. (Samuel Parker must have told him of William White's letter.) "The assertion, therefore, I confess, is a falsehood, but not of my framing. . . . I still cherish the hope that I shall receive ordination from your hands."[17]

On May 5, Provoost wrote to Freeman that it was not in his power to ordain him, given his beliefs, but suggested that Freeman might appeal to the next convention. On May 29, Freeman wrote to Provoost:

> I apply therefore to you, and through you to the Convention, in the name of the church at which I officiate, and humbly solicit that you and they would be pleased to relax at this point, and confer holy orders upon me, upon my subscribing to a declaration of faith in the sacred scriptures. . . . We wish to be considered as an Episcopal church, to throw our weight, whatever it is, into the Episcopal scale. . . . We admire the liturgy of the Church of England. At the same time however we do find some of the Book of Common Prayer exceptionable.
>
> We highly approve many parts of the Philadelphia liturgy [the unaccepted book of 1785]; we think the alterations judicious. We are willing to adopt several things in it, and to correct our Liturgy by it. But some prayers are still being retained which appear to us not altogether scriptural. . . . We beg that you would connect us by the ties of Episcopal ordination and the bonds of Charity, whilst you permit us to worship according to our consciences.
>
> We foresee that objections will be made to our request, but we cannot conceive what injury so liberal an extension of your plan can do the Episcopal cause. . . . We are determined to procure it [Episcopal ordination], if possible, and shall not, till we are repeatedly rejected, apply to any other source.[18]

Two days later Samuel Parker wrote to Bela Hubbard, "Mr. Freeman still continues at the Chapel Church, so called; his congregation is very small, and they uneasy at his not being able to obtain Orders. He has made an overture to Bishop Provoost on this head, and the matter, I hear, is to be the subject of discussion at a convocation to be held, or already held, at Philadelphia."[19]

Parker also wrote Seabury, and in his letter suggested that the bishop preach at King's Chapel. Seabury replied, "Your mention of the Chapel at Boston I consider mere banter, as I should suppose myself the last person in the States who would be invited thither, and that Church as the most unlikely, under the present situation, to suit my ideas of doctrine or discipline."[20]

On June 24 (or possibly July 1) William Montague, who had been a reader for eighteen months at Christ Church (the Old North) in Boston, was ordained by Bishop William White in Philadelphia. (Why was he not ordained by Seabury who was considerably closer?) After Montague returned to Boston with a report of the service, the Warden and Vestry decided again to apply to Provoost.

On July 29 they wrote to Provoost as follows:

We have long been deprived of the benefit of the ordinances of religion, and we feel the inconvenience, but we would consent to forego the advantages of them until the meeting of the Convention, if you could encourage us with any hope that the American church will acknowledge us as brethren, and agree to the ordination of our Minister, upon the terms which we submit. . . . We have reason to fear that our church has been misrepresented by our enemies to the Episcopal clergy of the Southern states. It has been suggested, we are told, that we are already dissatisfied with the new liturgy which we have adopted, that we do not wish our Minister should obtain Ordination, but are anxious to return to the book of common prayer of the church of England. We assure you . . . there is no ground for these insinuations.[21]

The authors of this letter then told Provoost that they had

heard that when Montague was ordained in Philadelphia, he had only to declare his faith in scripture and promise to conform to the doctrines and worship of the Protestant church in Massachusetts. (Had Montague himself told them this?) "In this state no doctrines or form of worship are yet established," said the letter. "Has not our Church therefore as good a claim to style itself the protestant Episcopal Church of Massachusetts as any other? . . . Is [it] not in your power to ordain Mr. Freeman on the same conditions as Mr. Montague? We are willing that he should make the same subscription, provided that he might be . . . allowed to use the Liturgy of this church, a copy of which we do ourselves the honour to present you. With anxiety we shall wait for any answer to this letter, and for your opinion upon the matters contained in it."[22]

Provoost's reply of August 13 settled all doubts as to what course King's Chapel should take. He told the Wardens that upon consulting several of his colleagues he found them "unanimously of the opinion that it would be improper for me to enter into a discussion of the business of your letter, as they think a subject of so much importance ought to be reserved entirely for the consideration of the general Convention. It is in compliance with their advice that I now refer you to the first meeting of that Assembly."[23]

This assembly, the first convention of both southern and northern delegates, was scheduled to meet in the next year, 1788. (It did not actually meet until October of 1789.)

By now, convinced that the bishops would not ordain Freeman in the near future, the Wardens, Vestry, and Proprietors of King's Chapel decided to ordain their reader independently of any other church or authority.

On October 30, 1787, a committee of Charles Miller, Perez Morton, and George Minot reported a plan for ordination to the Wardens and Vestry. They recommended that the church "ordain, constitute and appoint James Freeman to be their Minister with full power to Preach, Baptize, Administer the Holy Communion, Bury the Dead, and perform all the other Rites and Offices usually performed by a Minister in Episcopal orders. Let this vote be entered upon the Records of the

Church," they said. "Let it be read in Publick on Some Sunday Evening, after divine service. Let the Members of the church publickly signify their assent to it. And let Mr. Freeman Declare that he Accepts of this Ordination and Appointment."[24]

Their plan for ordination began with a long defense. The church leaders, it said, saw no immediate hope of securing episcopal ordination. They did not wish to follow what they called "presbyterian ordination," by which they meant an ordination sanctioned by the clergy and lay delegates of neighboring churches, gathered formally as a council.

This form of ordination, more commonly called "congregational," was followed by most Boston churches. In this procedure the clergy of neighboring churches offered the right hand of fellowship to the proposed minister, laid hands upon his head while he knelt, and prayed for him, and in other ways intimated that the authority for the ordination came not just from a single congregation but from the neighboring churches as well. Had King's Chapel used this form of ordination, so closely associated with Congregationalism, it would have shown (as Samuel Parker said some two years earlier) that King's Chapel had definitely left the Episcopal church and joined the Congregationalists. Clearly King's Chapel, by avoiding congregational ordination, showed that it still hoped at some time to find a bishop who would ordain their minister.

Since congregational ordination was not feasible at this time, the only mode of ordination left to King's Chapel was what was called independent ordination. The congregation itself would ordain Freeman without the presence or participation of bishop, priest, or minister. That is, they would ordain him without benefit of clergy.

In defense of this mode of ordination, the ordaining committee appealed to scripture, the practice of the early church, and the republican principles of a new nation. At the ordination itself the Wardens stated that they were acting on the basis of "the third article in the Declaration of Rights."

Specifically, the Senior Warden told the congregation at the ordination that the Vestry's and proprietors' authority to ordain rested on the third article in the Declaration of Rights in the recently enacted Massachusetts constitution. This article authorizes the legislature to require "towns, parishes, precincts, and other bodies politic, or religious societies" to provide for "the public worship of God and the support and maintenance of public Protestant teachers of piety, religion and morality." But Article III further stipulates that these bodies have "the exclusive right of electing their public teachers and of contracting with them for their support and maintenance." As a religious society, King's Chapel clearly had the right to elect and contract with James Freeman against the claims of any recently elected Episcopal bishop whose civil powers were still untested.

It is clear from this and from other statements made to justify the ordination of Freeman's successors that the church appealed as much to civil as to religious authority. In Peabody's installation the Wardens, Vestry, and Proprietors elected and ordained the ordinand "by virtue of the Constitution and Laws of this Commonwealth."[25] Subsequent clergy were ordained to the roles of pastor, preacher, teacher, and " . . . *to the other offices which of right belong to any minister by virtue of the authority of the laws and constitution of this Commonwealth* [my italics] with the usual addition of 'by virtue of our lawful authority.' "[26]

The committee's defense of independent ordination continued as follows:

> . . . common sense alone is sufficient to Vindicate the proposed plan of ordination in a case of necessity; and such, it cannot be denied, the present case is. Jesus Christ commanded his disciples to be baptized in his name of Religion, and to eat Bread and drink wine in Remembrance of him; these are Indispensable obligations. . . . It may be asked if a number of persons were cast onshore on a desolate Island, and cut off from all communication from the Rest of the World, would they think themselves under the necessity of renouncing Christianity? Would they not Institute a Church? Would they not preserve the forms of publick worship? Would they not appoint

one of their number to Instruct them in the Doctrines and precepts of the Gospel? . . . Can it be supposed that God would be displeased with them, if they did?"[27]

This appeal to common sense (coming directly from the Scottish philosophers in the 1770s) was the clincher. A bishop could give no special power. "A minister after Ordination remains exactly the same man as he was before. Ordination therefore is only a Decent human Institution. It is a Ceremony by which a Minister is introduced into office."[28] John Locke himself could not have put it better.

After hearing this plan and defense, the Vestry appointed from the congregation a committee of twelve to review it and report back in a week. The Vestry agreed that the ceremony should take place at Evening Prayer on Sunday, November 18, that a vote should be taken at that ceremony and entered into the church records. The committee of twelve suggested the wording for this vote, namely, that James Freeman was to become "Rector, Minister, Priest, Pastor, Teaching Elder and Public Teacher, and is to remain in full force so long as he shall continue to preach the word of God, and to dispense instructions of piety, religion and morality conformably to our opinions and sentiments of the Scriptures, and no longer."[29] This wording further stipulated that a three-fourths vote of the Wardens, Vestry, and Proprietors would be necessary in order to remove the Minister from office.

This meeting added a final and significant proviso: "It is further Voted that if at any time hereafter ordination by the imposition of hands from a Bishop in common and usual form can be obtained for Mr. Freeman without sacrificing our own religious sentiments to those of others, we will adopt that method in *confirmation* [my italics] of the present mode of ordination."[30]

This proviso was repeated in the ordinations of Freeman's two successors, Samuel Cary and Francis Greenwood. Furthermore, the prayer for bishops was kept in the next edition (1811) of the prayerbook. By 1828, however, when the church published the third edition, the legal battle with Trinity Church

over the Price estate had confirmed King's Chapel's separation
from other Episcopal churches, and the prayer for bishops was
dropped.

A week later the Committee of Twelve reported to the
Proprietors their pleasure with the plan and their conviction
that it was "warranted by the holy scriptures, by the practise of
the primitive christians, is consonant to the civil constitution
under which we live and that it is adequate to the present
exigencies of the church."[31]

On Friday, November 16, a protest against Freeman's ordination signed by seventeen Proprietors of the church was
delivered to the Senior Warden. The protest claimed that the
reader and leaders of the church had effectively abandoned
Episcopal faith, tradition, and practice by their liturgical innovations, and it declared the signers' "utter abhorrence of measures so contrary to the doctrine, discipline, and worship of an
Episcopal church . . . [representing] a total alienation of the
property of said house from the use intended by the original
founders or donors."[32]

The ordination proceeded despite the protest. On Sunday,
November 18, after the reading of Evening Prayer, the two
Wardens joined James Freeman at the reading desk and Dr.
Bulfinch, the senior of the two wardens, addressed the congre-
gation as follows:

> 1. Brethren of the church and congregation who statedly
> worship in this church, at your last meeting at this place,
> you appointed this day for the Ordination of the Rev. Mr.
> Freeman; you then determined it by a Vote which I shall
> read to be signed by the Wardens. But as this method of
> procedure may appear new and unprecedented to some
> of this Audience, it may not be amiss to assign a reason
> for adopting it.
>
> It is now upwards of four years since you made choice
> of the Rev. Mr. Freeman for your Minister, since which
> time you have been anxious for his Ordination, in order
> that he might be empowered to administer the ordi-
> nances of the Gospel—and although you have repeatedly

sought for this power, yet you have not been able to obtain it. Some hopes have been conceived, from the American Bishops, the right Reverend Dr. Seabury; and since, from the right Reverend Dr. Provoost, but that prospect being still distant, you have adopted the present, rather than being longer deprived of these Ordinances.[33]

There are two accounts of what happened next in the service. According to Francis Greenwood's history, the Senior Warden announced that Mr. Freeman would lead the congregation in prayer, and he did so. But this is contradicted by two documents, recently rediscovered at the Massachusetts Historical Society. One, entitled "A Plan of Ordination for Mr. Freeman," stipulates that the Senior Warden should at this point read aloud the protest against Freeman's ordination. Since the protest was delivered to the Senior Warden on Friday, November 16, this plan of ordination must have been drawn up on that day or the following day. This was, therefore, in all likelihood the last plan of ordination that the Wardens and Vestry drew up.

The second document, entitled "Minutes of the Reverend Mr. Freeman's Ordination," appears to be a record of the proceeding written during the service. Like the first document, this one indicates that after his opening remarks the Senior Warden read the protest of the dissenters. Penciled handwriting on the document entitled "The Plan" states that James Freeman later thought that the protest was *not* read and that Joseph May thought it *was*. Greenwood's account of the service relies on Freeman's memory. I have preferred to trust the testimony of these two documents and the memory of Joseph May. I believe that the latter's memory is well attested to in the deposition that he delivered in the court case over the Price estate. (In 1770 William Price had left to King's Chapel his house on Cornhill. Subsequently this became the subject of three court cases. In the final disposition of the case, King's Chapel and Trinity Church now share the income from this estate, which also supports the annual Price Lectures administered by Trinity Church.)

According, then, to the plan and the minutes at this point in the service the Senior Warden said:

> From the unanimity which appeared at your last meeting, we conceived hopes, that we should meet with no interruption in our proposed plan; but unhappily some of our Brethren who have lately withdrawn from us, and joined themselves to other Churches, and who consequently do not belong to this Congregation, cannot approve of the method which we are about to take, and have signified their Dissent, by way of a protest—the number of those signing the protest is 17. As however the majority of Votes is in favor of ordination, it is presumed we may lawfully proceed, lamenting the nonconcurrence of our Brethren, wishing them at the same time every Christian comfort in the enjoyment of their religious Sentiments. This protest, to show our impartiality, although it has been desired, we will now proceed to read.[34]
>
> 2. Whereas certain persons calling themselves proprietors of the Stone Chapel in Boston have of late declared that the pews of a number of the original proprietors are forfeit on account of their absence, and have sold said pews to persons who never were of the Episcopal Church, and who hold sentiments diametrically opposite to said Church; and said new proprietors have introduced a Liturgy, different from any now used in the Episcopal churches in the United States, and articles of faith which in our opinion are unscriptural and heretical; and have thereby deprived many of the proprietors of said house of their property and the privilege of worshipping God therein according to the dictates of their consciences; and whereas we are informed by a Committee from said proprietors that they intend, next Lord's day, to take upon themselves to authorize Mr. James Freeman to administer the sacraments of baptism and the Lord's Supper in said church, and to receive him as a regular ordained Minister, which step in our opinion is unprecedented, irregular, and contrary to apostolic and primi-

tive usage, and to the common sentiments of almost every sect and denomination of Christians, a step which may be attended with fatal consequences to the interests of religion in general and that of the Episcopal Church in particular, we therefore the subscribers, in behalf of ourselves and other original proprietors of this church, who have authorized us to act for them, do hereby enter our most solemn and serious protest and dissent against all such proceedings, and particularly against the settlement and pretended ordination of the said James Freeman, declaring our utter abhorrence of the measures so contrary to the doctrine, discipline, and worship of an Episcopal church, and which will include in them a total alienation of the property of said house from the use intended by the original donors or founders.

JAMES IVERS for himself and James Trecothick, Esq., GILBERT DEBLOIS, for himself, Lewis Deblois, and Henry Leddell, JAMES LLOYD, for Wm. Vassall, Esqr. HENRY SMITH, for Henry Lloyd. JAMES APTHORP. CHARLES WILLIAMS. THEODORE DEHON. JOHN BOX. JOHN HASKINS. LYDIA BOX. MATTHEW NAZRO. AMBROSE VINCENT. GRIZZELL APTHORP. DOROTHY FORBES.[35]

The manuscript entitled "A Plan for the Ordination for Mr. Freeman" includes the following paragraph, which is crossed out (the Senior Warden may or may not have read it):

2. Brethren, I have read the protest of those persons who disapprove of the business we are engaging in. The meaning and spirit of it, being plain and unequivocal, needs no comment. You will however observe that of the 17 signing the protest—five persons, from their local situation, can never be expected to worship in this country at all,— ten of the others have long since withdrawn from us; so that we have, properly speaking, only 2 persons who may be said to dissent, Viz. Mr. Vincent and Madame Apthorp,

whose loss we greatly lament.[36]

The Senior Warden then said:

3. Brethren, as the Business in which we are now to engage is of a most serious and important nature, it becomes us to begin it with a solemn address to Almighty God, the great parent of mankind.

Here James Freeman read the first ordaining prayer and the Senior Warden then said:

4. We the Warden, vestry, proprietors and congregation of King's Chapel, or First Episcopal Church in Boston, do by virtue of the third article in the Declaration of Rights hereby solemnly elect, ordain, constitute, and appoint the Rev. James Freeman of said Boston, to be our Rector, Minister, Public Teacher, Priest, Pastor, and teaching Elder, to preach the Word of God, and to dispense lessons and instructions in piety, religion, and morality; and to minister the holy sacraments in the congregation; and to do, perform, and discharge all other duties and offices which of right belong to any other Rector, minister, public teacher, Pastor, teaching elder or Priest in orders.

And it is hereby understood and intended that the authority and rights hereby given to the said James Freeman to be our Rector, Minister, public Teacher, Priest, and teaching Elder and Pastor, are to remain in full force so long as he shall continue to preach the word of God, and dispense instructions in piety, religion, and morality, conformably to our opinions and sentiments of the Holy Scriptures and no longer; and that our judgement of his not thus conforming to our religious sentiments and opinions shall be ascertained by the votes of three fourths of the Wardens and vestry, and of three fourths of the proprietors usually worshipping in said church, separately and individually taken.

5. Brethren, if this vote be agreeable to your mind, if you readily and cheerfully adopt it, if you mean to convey all the powers expressed in it, please to testify it.

In token of their unanimous approbation, the proprietors lifted up their right hands. (The Senior Warden then said:)

"If it is your desire that the said vote be now signed by the Wardens in your behalf, please to testify it."

6. The Proprietors, as before, unanimously lifted up their right hands.

7. The Senior Warden then addressing Mr. Freeman, said:

"Reverend Sir, it appears by the vote in favor of your ordination that you are lawfully chosen; it is expected that you now declare your acceptance of the choice."

Mr. Freeman then read and presented to the Senior Warden the following subscribed by him; *viz.*, "To the Wardens, Vestry, Proprietors, and Congregation of the Chapel, of the First Episcopal Church in Boston. Brethren, with cheerfulness and gratitude I accept your election and ordination, which I believe to be valid and apostolick. And I pray God to enable me to preach the word, and to administer the ordinances of religion in such a manner, as that I may promote his glory, the honour of the great Redeemer, and your spiritual edification. (signed) James Freeman. November 18, 1787."

The Senior Warden then delivered to Mr. Freeman a copy of the ordaining vote, signed by the Wardens; and laying his hand on Mr. Freeman, said:

"I do then, as Senior Warden of this church, by virtue of the authority delegated to me in the presence of Almighty God and before these witnesses, declare to you, the Rev. James Freeman, to be the Rector, Minister,

Priest, Pastor, public Teacher, and teaching Elder of this Episcopal church; in testimony whereof I deliver you this book [delivering him a Bible], containing the holy oracles of Almighty God, enjoining a due observance of all the precepts contained therein, particularly those which respect the duty and office of a Minister of Jesus Christ. And the Lord bless you and keep you, the Lord lift up the light of his countenance upon you, and give you peace now and for evermore." The whole Assembly, as one man spontaneously and emphatically pronounced Amen.[37]

9. James Freeman then read a second ordaining prayer.

10. The Senior Warden then said: "Brethren, we have now finished the business which called us together. Nothing remains, but that we receive this our pastor with that cordial affection which is due to his office. And remember that however widely different the sentiments of Christians of different persuasions may be, yet that all those who truly fear God and work righteousness, shall be accepted of him."[38]

According to Greenwood's account, the second ordaining prayer was followed by an anthem and a sermon on the duties and offices of a Christian minister preached, of course, by James Freeman. Another anthem concluded the service.

On the day after the ceremony Freeman wrote to Theophilus Lindsey:

[T]ired of delay and disgusted with the narrowness of mind which the American bishops have discovered, they have recognized those rights which reason and Christianity give them. They have determined to ordain me themselves, according to a plan first suggested by Governor Bowdoin, a gentleman whose learning, good sense and merit give a sanction to any sentiment which he endorses. Yesterday the ceremony was performed . . .

with great decency and solemnity, in the presence of a very numerous assembly. Deep attention was impressed upon every countenance, and many of the advocates for religious liberty of our own and other churches could not forbear expressing their sensibility by tears of joy.

The vote respecting the ordination by the Bishop was passed in tenderness to the prejudices of a few persons, who, though they are liberal in other respects, still believe that some virtue is conveyed by the hands of a prelate. I confess I do not like it, but I flatter myself that my worthy friends who have any scruples left, will soon be [unclear] of them; for it appears to me that a very little reflection is sufficient to convince them that the essence of ordination consists in the choice of the people and that no foreign authority is necessary.[39]

Freeman later wrote to his father of the event, stating "After being refused ordination by the Bishops Seabury and Provoost, at which refusal I inwardly rejoiced, the Wardens and Vestry . . . in consequence of a paper which I laid before them, . . . unanimously voted to ordain me themselves."[40]

The first newspaper to report the event was *The Independent Chronicle*, which printed in its "Boston" column, "Last Sunday afternoon, the Reverend Mr. James Freeman was ordained to the pastoral charge of the first Episcopal church in this town. The ceremony was performed with propriety and seriousness, in presence of a prodigious crowd of spectators."[41]

In the next column appeared the protest of the dissident proprietors with this note in italics at the head, "As the mode of inducting Mr. Freeman into the ministerial office on the last Lord's Day at the Stone Chapel in this town, was certainly very singular, if not wholly unprecedented: And lest it should appear to the world, that the transaction was unanimously pleasing to the proprietors of that church, you are requested to publish the following dissent which was presented to the Senior Warden. . . ."[42]

William Bentley wrote to his friend and colleague in Boston: "My dear friend, This moment I have received by the

Salem Gazette (November 26) the glorious news of your Triumph over an oppressive enemy—It has raised me into a transport—Have you leisure enough for a friend to give me a few circumstances. God bless you—you have kept the faith, your affectionate friend, etc."[43]

Then commenced the battle of the newspapers. In answer to the protests of the seventeen disaffected Proprietors, the Wardens and Vestry printed their rebuttal. Five dissenters, they argued, were nonresidents and voted through proxies. How could they judge of the situation in King's Chapel? Three dissenters had worshiped at Trinity since 1775, another had not attended worship at the Chapel for several years, and two had actually voted for the alterations to the liturgy. Not one of the twenty-four Old Proprietors or twenty new ones had protested. The Wardens defended the prayerbook revisions as scriptural and their proceedings as legal.

A self-styled "spectator" wrote this to the *Centinel*:

On Sunday last appeared at the Stone Chapel the most wonderful of all phenomena that this, or any other country, ever produced: Before the eyes of a gaping multitude was exhibited an Empirick, invested with the sacerdotal powers, and by a bailiff ceremony of a clap on the shoulder, calling to the priesthood an aspiring follower of the crack-brained Lindsey; bowed his astonished head in token of his unblushing readiness to receive the full emoluments of marriage, christenings, and burials; then was the infidel hand raised in triumph, whilst the insulted eye of Christianity sunk to the earth: All distinction was levelled with the dust, and that sacred building which was formerly consecrated to order and propriety, disgraced by the projects of an irreligious junto and an ambitious sectary.[44]

A rejoinder to this in the same issue was entitled "A Rowland for your Oliver" and read as follows:

On Sunday the 18th instant was exhibited at the house

formerly called the king's chapel, an instance of the publick exercise of a long dormant right, which every society civil and religious, has to elect and ORDAIN their own officers. . . . Invested with this right by the God of nature—secured in the exercise of it by the civil constitution, and encouraged by the approbation of all the consistent friends of order and liberty, the independent congregation . . . publickly invested with the ministerial office, a sensible honest man; who publickly accepted the Bible, as the only standard of his faith, and directory of his preaching and ministrations. Thus without any mysterious and unintelligible ceremonies—without any assumption of apostolick powers—without any pretended superiority of office—without any affected communication of sacerdotal effluvia, was a servant of Jesus Christ introduced to his office, in a style, simple, decent, primitive and constitutional.

Thus was cut the aspiring comb of political pride;—then was undermined the pompous fabrick of hierarchical usurpations; then was pricked the puffed bladder of uninterrupted succession;—while the eye of liberty sparkled with joy, and the modest face of primitive, simple, unadulterated Christianity brightened with the conscious smile of a decent, manly, substantial triumph![45]

A satire, entitled "Writ de Haeretico Comburnendo," appeared later in the *Centinel.* Purporting to be by Samuel Parker and the American bishops, it ordered the arrest and public burning of James Freeman, the Wardens, Vestry, and congregation of King's Chapel because of their heresy and rebellion against Episcopal authority.[46]

This satire, characteristic of Puritan anti-Episcopal invective in Boston newspapers, was a response to the protest lodged against Freeman's ordination in December 1787 by the Episcopal clergy in and around Boston, which read as follows:

Whereas a certain Congregation in Boston, calling themselves the first Episcopal Church in said town, have, in an irregular and unconstitutional manner, introduced a Liturgy essentially differing from any used in the Episcopal Churches in this Commonwealth and in the United States, not to mention the Protestant Episcopal Church in general; and have also assumed to themselves a power, unprecedented in said Church, of separating to the work of the Ministry Mr. James Freeman, who has for some time past been their Reader, and of themselves have authorized or pretendedly authorized him to administer the Sacraments of Baptism and the Lord's Supper, and at the same time most inconsistently and absurdly take to themselves the name and style of an Episcopal Church, . . .

We, the Ministers of the Protestant Episcopal Church, whose names are underwritten, do hereby declare the proceedings of said Congregation, usually meeting at the Stone Chapel in Boston, to be irregular, unconstitutional, diametrically opposite to every principle adopted in any Episcopal Church; subversive of all order and regularity, and pregnant with Consequences fatal to the Interests of Religion. And we do hereby, and in this public manner, protest against the aforesaid Proceedings, to the end that all those of our Communion, wherever dispersed, may be cautioned against receiving said Reader, or Preacher (Mr. James Freeman) as a clergyman of our Church, of holding Communion with him as such, and may be induced to look upon his Congregation in the light in which it ought to be looked upon by all true Episcopalians.

EDWARD BASS
Saint Paul's Church, Newburyport

NATHANIEL FISHER
Saint Peter's Church, Salem

SAMUEL PARKER
Trinity Church, Boston

THOMAS FITCH OLIVER
Saint Michael's Church, Marblehead

WILLIAM MONTAGUE
Christ's Church, Boston

JOHN C. OGDEN
Queen's Chapel, Portsmouth, N.H.

December, 1787[47]

Samuel Parker, rector of Trinity Church, had organized this protest. As the text shows plainly, he wanted the Boston public to understand that although the new American Episcopal church was unorganized, it would allow no priests to be ordained except by a bishop. Parker believed that the new American Episcopal church must be known as a church governed by bishops and could permit no independent or congregational authority.

Not all of the Episcopal clergy signed Parker's protest. Willard Wheeler of Scituate wrote to Parker that it was better to ignore the ordination than to publicize it and elicit sympathy for King's Chapel. He told Parker that the proceedings should be treated with "silent contempt" and that the absurdity of King's Chapel styling itself "Episcopal" would soon expose them to ridicule.

As Wheeler guessed, Freeman was delighted by the protest and the ensuing publicity. "In order to manifest my contempt of it," he wrote to his father, "I published it in one of our newspapers."[48] A few months later he wrote, "I now consider myself as upon so firm a basis that I cannot be shaken. Every murmur of censure has long since died away and the publick, as well as my friends, view me as a regularly ordained minister." He then adds, ". . . almost all the religious societies in Boston are remarkably catholick. The several sects live together in the utmost harmony; the consequence of our knowledge, and the free constitution of government under which we have the happiness to live."[49]

Freeman then told his father that he had joined the local association of Congregational clergy some years ago and hoped to exchange pulpits with them. In fact, however, he exchanged just once with William Bentley[50] and possibly once with John Eckley of Old South, but enjoyed no exchanges beyond these and took no part in the ordinations of his colleagues.

Some years later Bentley wrote of him, "He much declines preaching abroad, after the warmest solicitations. He preached by change of pulpit many years ago and has not exchanged in that manner since. His peculiar situation with the Liturgy and Church has placed him in a separate state so that no intercourse with him can be direct."[51]

The reason for Freeman's isolation was probably not the indifference of the Boston clergy but the hope of some, or many, members of King's Chapel for episcopal ordination. They and Freeman knew that if he fraternized excessively with the Congregationalists, he would lose any chance of being ordained by a bishop. Freeman, though hardly sympathetic to their hopes, acceded to them, and thus assumed the entire burden of preaching at his church without the relief of a regular, or even occasional, exchange.

Freeman continued to be on good terms with his colleagues and fellow citizens. "All the Congregational ministers in Boston have on this occasion treated me with great friendship. . . . Judge Cushing in particular has publickly declared that such an ordination as mine is valid and constitutional. And what is of more importance the Convention of Massachusetts who have assembled for the purpose of ratifying the constitution proposed by the Federal Convention, have acknowledged me to be an ordained minister by inviting me to officiate in my turn as their chaplain with the other ministers of Boston."[52]

It was in this way that James Freeman became so ensconced in the heart of King's Chapel and the church itself was so completely accepted by Boston society that in the next century it successfully withstood two court challenges, one from Trinity Church and one from the Episcopal diocese, to its share in the inheritance of William Price.

One can see in retrospect why ordination was so important

to Freeman and the congregation. In the first place, despite Freeman's private reservations, there was no question in the congregation's mind that he should be ordained before he married, buried, baptized, or celebrated communion. We have no record of Freeman's performing any of those ceremonies until after November 18, 1787.[53]

Secondly, the congregation's right to choose its own leader assumed its right to exist independently of the authority of bishops or other congregations. Although Trinity Church and the diocese challenged it, the courts of the Commonwealth upheld King's Chapel's right to define its own liturgy and choose its own minister. The right to emend the prayerbook and ordain its own clergy meant essentially the right to survive.

If the church and minister had not continued in their resolve, King's Chapel today would be but one of six Episcopal churches within a square mile of each other in downtown Boston. We would be using the 1978 Episcopal prayerbook in place of our own liturgy. We would have no chance to make our Christian witness among the churches and fellowships of the Unitarian Universalist Association. Indeed, given the competition between so many similar churches in a small area, we might not exist at all.

We should appreciate the delicate and essential balance of power between James Freeman and the lay leaders of this church. If the laity had not checked his zeal in revising the liturgy, we might have gone the way of so many congregationally governed churches and given up our prayerbook through a process of gradual attrition. On the other hand, if Freeman had not pressed the laity to reform the liturgy, they would probably never have initiated so momentous a task. It was the ability of both clergy and laity to exercise their separate but complementary powers that enabled us to find our curious and not insignificant place in American religious history.

Notes

1. William Stevens Perry, *The History of the American Episcopal Church* (Boston: James R. Osgood & Co., 1885), p. 45.
2. James Freeman to William White, January 8, 1786, Collection at Houghton Library (hereafter referred to as HL), Harvard University, Cambridge, MA.
3. Quoted in Marion Hatchet, "The Making of the First American Prayerbook," submitted in partial fulfillment of the requirements for the degree of Doctor of Theology in the General Theological Seminary, New York, New York, February 1, 1972, p. 97.
4. *Ibid.*
5. Samuel Parker to William White, January 31, 1786, in *Seabury Traditions, The Reconstructed Journal of Connecticut's Diocesan*, Vol. 2, ed. Kenneth Walter Cameron (Hartford: Transcendental Books, 1983), p. 23. The letter continues: "Indeed the Minority is more properly the Majority. For in order to carry their point the first Step was to declare the pews of the Absentees, of which Description of Persons were a great number of the Proprietors of that most elegant Church, to be confiscated or forfeited. They then passed a Vote that no Person shd have liberty to purchase a Vault under the church (of which there were a number unappropriated) who was not a Proprietor of the church. These vaults being in great demand induced many Dissenters to become Proprietors for the sake of being entitled to a Vault, & they, tho they do not attend the Worship of the church, were called in to vote for adopting this new Liturgy. But a very few of the old proprietors are now attendants there but the greater number are Dissenters, the most thorough paced one of all is their Reader. I am told that an Answer to your letter is gone forward in the name I suppose of Mr. Miller but the joint Production of the whole Committee consisting of Lawyers Doctors Merchants & Mechanics with Mr. Freeman at their head. But magna est Veritas et prevalebit."
6. The Wardens and Vestry of King's Chapel to Samuel Seabury, February 7, 1786, in Henry Wilder Foote, "James Freeman and King's Chapel," *The Religious Magazine and Monthly Review*, June 1873, *49*(6):516.
7. James Freeman to Constant Freeman, October 31, 1786, Foote, "James Freeman and King's Chapel," p. 518.
8. Samuel Seabury to Thomas Bulfinch, May 29, 1786, in archives at King's Chapel Parish House, Boston, MA.
9. Cameron, *Seabury Traditions*, p. 30.

10. Nathaniel Fisher to James Freeman, as quoted in "Address by James Freeman Clarke," *The Centenary of the King's Chapel Liturgy* (Boston: Press of George H. Ellis, 1885) p. 27.

11. James Freeman to Constant Freeman, October 31, 1786, quoted in James Freeman Clarke, "James Freeman, D.D.," *Sprague's Annals of the American Pulpit*, Vol. 8:166-167.

12. Samuel Parker to William White, September 15, 1786, *The Correspondence of Samuel Parker*, ed. Kenneth Walter Cameron, (Hartford, CT: Transcendental Books, 1984), p. 21.

13. William White to Samuel Parker, October 14, 1786, p. 4, Collection of the Massachusetts Historical Society (hereafter referred to as MHS).

14. Ezra Stiles, *Literary Diary*, Vol. 3, ed. Kenneth Walter Cameron, pp. 234-235.

15. *Ibid.*

16. James Freeman to Constant Freeman, October 31, 1786, HL.

17. James Freeman to Samuel Provoost, April 19, 1787, MHS.

18. James Freeman to Samuel Provoost, May 29, 1787, MHS.

19. Samuel Parker to Bela Hubbard, June 1, 1787, quoted in Cameron, *The Correspondence of Samuel Parker*, p. 23.

20. Samuel Seabury to Samuel Parker, June 5, 1787, quoted in Cameron, *Seabury Traditions*, p. 43.

21. The Wardens and Vestry of King's Chapel to Samuel Provoost, August 13, 1787, as quoted in Francis William Pitt Greenwood, *A History of King's Chapel* (Boston: Carter Hendee & Co., 1833), pp. 181-182.

22. *Ibid.*

23. Samuel Provoost to the Wardens and Vestry of King's Chapel, August 13, 1787, quoted in Greenwood, *A History of King's Chapel*, p. 183.

24. Records of the Wardens and Vestry of King's Chapel, October 30, 1787, MHS.

25. *Annals of King's Chapel*, eds. Henry Edes and Henry Wilder Foote (Boston: Little Brown, 1896), Vol. 2, p. 497.

26. Descriptions of these ordinations may be found in Vol. 2 and Vol. 3 of Edes and Foote, *Annals*.

27. Records of the Wardens and Vestry of King's Chapel, October 30, 1787, MHS.

28. *Ibid.*

29. Records of the Wardens and Vestry of King's Chapel, November 4, 1787, MHS.

30. *Ibid.*

31. Records of the Proprietors of Pews of King's Chapel, November 11, 1787, MHS.
32. Greenwood, *A History of King's Chapel*, pp. 184-185.
33. *Ibid.*, pp. 192-195.
34. "A Plan of Ordination for Mr. Freeman," King's Chapel Archives, MHS.
35. Greenwood, *A History of King's Chapel*, pp. 184-185.
36. "A Plan of Ordination for Mr. Freeman," King's Chapel Archives, MHS.
37. Greenwood, *A History of King's Chapel*, pp. 192-195.
38. "A Plan of Ordination for Mr. Freeman," King's Chapel Archives, MHS.
39. James Freeman to Theophilus Lindsey, November 19, 1787, Collection of Doctor Williams's Library, 10 Gordon Square, London (hereafter referred to as DWL).
40. James Freeman to Constant Freeman, February 7, 1788, HL.
41. *The Independent Chronicle*, November 22, 1787, Boston Public Library (hereafter referred to as BPL).
42. *Ibid.*
43. "Address by James Freeman Clarke," *The Centenary of the King's Chapel Liturgy* (Boston: Press of George H. Ellis, 1885), p. 28.
44. *The Centinel*, November 28, 1787, p. 2, BPL.
45. *Ibid.*, According to Greenwood's history (pp. 142 and 195) the author of this piece was Jeremy Belknap, called only in January 1787 to the church in Long Lane, later called the Federal Street Church (where Channing preached) and then the Arlington Street Church.
46. *Massachusetts Centinel*, January 12, 1788, BPL. "As the minister of the Stone Chapel, and 'the congregation usually meeting' there, do persist in condemning the authority of their mother church, as declared in the late thunder of excommunication, and do still continue in the abominable sin of worshipping GOD according to the dictates of their own consciences; it will be necessary for the Church further to exercise their power, and to inflict such punishment as has been heretofore ordained for the such obstinate Hereticks. I have, therefore, for the benefit of the Bishops of the Convocation transcribed the ancient rite of burning of Hereticks and formed it for the present case. . . . We command you, and strictly injoin it upon you, that the aforesaid James Freeman, and the Wardens, Vestry, and congregation aforesaid, being in your custody in some publick and open place within your precinct, for the cause above alleged, in presence of the people you commit into a publick fire, and that in the

same fire you cause the said James Freeman, Wardens, Vestry and the congregation aforesaid, to be burned and consumed, in detestation of this horrid crime, and as a publick example to other Christians. . . ."

47. Greenwood, *A History of King's Chapel*, pp. 197-198.
48. Quoted in Henry Wilder Foote, "James Freeman and King's Chapel," p. 527.
49. James Freeman to Constant Freeman, August 30, 1788, HL.
50. William Bentley, *The Diary of William Bentley* (Gloucester, MA: Peter Smith, 1962), Vol. *1*, entry for October 26, 1788. "I exchanged with Mr. Freeman of King's Chapel, the first instance of this ministerial service with and without liturgies."
51. Bentley, *Diary*, Vol. 3, entry for July 3, 1804.
52. James Freeman to Constant Freeman, February 7, 1788, HL.
53. The records of King's Chapel at the MHS show that James Freeman performed his first baptism on December 31, 1787 (the first recorded since February 18, 1777), his first burial on January 2, 1788 (the first recorded since February 17, 1776), and his first marriage on May 27, 1788 (the first recorded since February 18, 1776).

FOUR

King's Chapel: Transition Toward Unitarianism

*An account of how King's Chapel became a different sort
of church: Anglican in worship, unitarian in thought,
and independent in polity.*

The oldest endowed chair in America is the Hollis Professor-ship of Divinity, established in Harvard College in 1721 by the will of Thomas Hollis, a London merchant. Harvard, in the eighteenth century, had become identified with moderate Calvinism and with the liberal Arminians (discussed in the first chapter). When Professor David Tappan, incumbent of the Hollis Chair, and a moderate Calvinist, died in 1803, Henry Ware, distinguished minister of Hingham's First Parish, was chosen as his successor. Widely regarded as the strongest candidate for the position, he was, nevertheless, known to be counted among the liberals. His contentious election as Hollis Professor in 1805 precipitated the Unitarian Controversy that was to divide the churches of the Standing Order in New England.

Liberal thought had flourished for half a century and some of the pillar doctrines of Calvinism, including ideas of original sin and eternal punishment, had been openly contested for a generation or more. Furthermore, by the last quarter of the century it was not uncommon to find clergy who had ceased to make any reference in their sermons to the doctrine of the Trinity. They held Arian views of the nature of Christ, subor-dinating the Son to the Father. A story is told of the Reverend

Thomas Barnard of Salem's North Church, a friend of James Freeman. A parishioner one day approached him and said, "Dr. Barnard, I never heard you preach a sermon upon the Trinity." His reply was decisive: "And you never will."

The election of Henry Ware to the Hollis Professorship was followed by the naming of another liberal, Samuel Webber, as President of the College in 1806; the two events signaled that the liberals had captured Harvard in what historian Samuel Eliot Morison called "a college revolution." In 1812, Andover Seminary was founded by a group of orthodox clergy in response to the growing power of the liberals at Harvard. Andover was to become the bastion of Calvinist theology and was to stand by the faith of the founders of the churches of New England.

In the same year a divisive blow was struck when John Codman, minister of the Second Church in Dorchester, refused to exchange pulpits with liberal clergy. The long-standing custom of the monthly pulpit exchange had been a significant symbol of unity. Codman's action shocked many people who saw it as the first rent in the fellowship of the churches of the Standing Order, the triumph of a new spirit of sectarianism. The lines between the orthodox and liberal parties were rapidly being drawn; separation was the inevitable result.

Unitarianism began as a biblical religion. While Unitarians acknowledged that certain basic religious truths, such as the existence of God, may be established by the use of reason, God's plan for the salvation of human souls is made known to us through revelation, the record of which is to be found in the pages of the Bible. Hence the science of biblical criticism was regarded by the liberal Christians as central in the theological training of the minister.

During the eighteenth century, Americans were familiar with the methods of biblical criticism and exegesis available to them in British works, but German critical scholarship was virtually unknown to them. It was just as the Unitarian Controversy was developing that American liberals became aware of the work done by such scholars as Michaelis and Griesbach. They seized on it eagerly because its conclusions promised to support them in their debates with the orthodox. After all, the chief argument against the doctrine of the Trinity was that it was unscriptural. A correct understanding of the Bible, they were confident, would assure the triumph of liberal Christianity.[1]

Joseph Buckminster was responsible for introducing German biblical scholarship to the American scene. A native of Portsmouth, New Hampshire, where he was born in 1784, the young Buckminster early showed a precociousness in the study of languages. He began Latin at the age of four, and the next year took up the study of Greek. Graduating from Harvard College at the age of sixteen, he had not only distinguished himself in the study of the classics, but had gained a working knowledge of Hebrew and French as well. He taught classics at Exeter for two years and at the same time began reading for the ministry. He then moved to Waltham where he was employed as a tutor. Here he came under the influence of James Freeman, commenced attending services at King's Chapel, and soon declared himself to be an Arian in Christology. He was invited to assist Dr. Freeman but declined. In 1804 he was ordained by Brattle Street Church shortly before his twenty-first birthday.

Within two years Buckminster's health began to fail, and his congregation sent him to Europe for a year of travel and rest. At the end of 1806 he returned to Boston with a collection of some 3,000 books, constituting the most scholarly and privately held library in New England. This library was to provide the tools for Buckminster's subsequent work in biblical criticism. By all counts his single most important acquisition was Griesbach's critical edition of the Greek New Testament. In 1807 Harvard College undertook the first American printing of Griesbach's Greek text with Buckminster himself correcting the proofs.[2]

Buckminster's influence and the ensuing ferment that the new criticism produced in the field of New Testament studies had a direct bearing on the thinking of William Ellery Channing (1780-1842). Channing preached his most famous sermon, "Unitarian Christianity," in Baltimore in 1819. He began with a clear definition of scripture and then proceeded to state the principles and methods to be used in the study of the Bible. Let me just mention two of them: first, that the Scriptures are not inspired, rather they contain the records of inspired men and women; second, Scripture must be interpreted by reason.[3]

This sermon, which Charles Lyttle called the Pentecost of American Unitarianism, became the foundation document for the liberal party. It is hard to imagine the extent of its impact. It has been said that its circulation was surpassed only by Tom Paine's *Common Sense*. Within six weeks five editions of the sermon had appeared. Translated into several languages and constantly reprinted, it must surely be counted among the greatest sermons to have been preached from any pulpit in America.

Six years later, in 1825, the American Unitarian Association was organized. What was the extent of James Freeman's participation in these events? And what role was King's Chapel to play in the ensuing story? It is to these questions that we turn now.

Harvard College conferred upon James Freeman the degree of Doctor of Divinity in 1811, the same year that marks the beginning of the Harvard Divinity School. In 1816 Freeman journeyed to Baltimore where he preached with the result that a church was formed there. In 1818, one year before Channing was to preach his great sermon, Freeman was back in Baltimore to give a sermon at the dedication of the new church erected by the congregation "for the maintenance of Unitarian and anti-Calvinistic worship." We know, too, that Freeman was frequently cited for his influence on younger ministers. He was interested in them, and he offered them his friendship. He was regarded, too, as something of an elder statesman by the generation of clergy and laity that founded the American Unitarian Association. Channing, we must remember, was Freeman's junior by twenty-one years.

In spite of the fact that Freeman was retired and in very frail health, he attended the founding meeting of the American Unitarian Association at the Federal Street Church and was, indeed, one of the signers of its constitution. His death came ten years later.

Freeman edited *Psalms and Hymns for Public Worship* in 1799. The collection included some one hundred and fifty-five psalms, chiefly taken from Tate and Brady, ninety hymns, and eight doxologies. It must have served King's Chapel well, for it was used for thirty-one years. Freeman wrote at least one hymn, "Lord of the Worlds Below," which he included in his *Psalms and Hymns* and which frequently found a place in collections of hymns throughout the nineteenth century. Fortunately, it appears in the latest edition of the King's Chapel prayerbook and so is once more available to us. It shows the influence of James Thomson's *The Seasons*. The first stanza is:

> Lord of the worlds below!
> On earth thy glories shine;
> The changing seasons show
> Thy skill and power divine.
> In all we see
> A God appears;
> The rolling years
> Are full of thee.[4]

I do not know if Freeman's hymnal was used outside King's Chapel, but it was the beginning of a tradition of hymnody at King's Chapel that would have an impact on the life of a larger circle of liberal Christian churches in the years that followed.

Dr. Scovel has shown that Freeman was a Socinian and thus more radical than the congregation of King's Chapel, which could be described as Arian. Arian, too, would be the most likely label for most of his colleagues. In Sprague's *Annals* there is a quotation that I find significant in describing something of the spirituality of Freeman: "He looked upon death, as it approached him, without fear, yet with pious humility. He viewed the last change as the most solemn change; the judgment of God upon the soul as the most solemn judgment. 'Let no man say when I am dead,' so he expressed himself to his nearest friends, 'I trusted in my own merits, I trust only in the mercy of God through Jesus Christ.' "[5]

The ministry of Samuel Cary, from 1809 to 1815, needs

passing mention. He was Dr. Freeman's colleague and was remembered for his work in catechizing and for the marked increase in the number of younger communicants as a result of his efforts. The second edition of the prayerbook, which appeared in 1811, was Cary's work. In the judgment of some people, the changes were not always for the best, and some of his alterations were eliminated from subsequent editions. He was a Socinian and was influenced by the more radical English Unitarianism of the day. The close bond of affection that existed between Freeman and Cary was pleasing to the congregation and no doubt helped to make the more radical ideas of the younger man more palatable to them. Evidence of his affection for his elder colleague is to be seen in the fact that he named his first son James Freeman Cary. Cary's untimely death left Freeman once more without assistance, a situation that existed for some nine years until 1824 when William Pitt Greenwood was settled as Freeman's colleague and successor.

Greenwood was born in Boston in 1797. His parents were members of King's Chapel, and it was here that he was baptized by James Freeman and shaped by its liturgy and its catechism. He graduated from Harvard College in 1814 and from the Divinity School three years later, just two years before Channing was to preach his famous Baltimore sermon. Greenwood thus belonged to the first generation of ministers active in the formation of the American Unitarian Association. His part in its life and work was considerable. A careful study has yet to be made of Greenwood's influence on the formation of the Association. Such a study is needed to come to some adequate understanding of the mutual relations forged between the oldest Unitarian church in America and the newly organized Unitarian Association.

Ordained in 1818 to the ministry of Boston's New South Church, Greenwood suffered his first attack of tuberculosis the following year. He resigned his pulpit and went south in an effort to regain his health. In due time he was settled in Baltimore and assisting Jared Sparks. (It was at Sparks's ordination in Baltimore that Channing preached "Unitarian Christianity.") At this time, too, Francis Greenwood married Maria

Goodwin. Baltimore agreed with him, so that he regained some of his health and was able to accept an invitation to assume part-time responsibilities at King's Chapel as assistant to James Freeman. After two years Freeman's health forced him to retire from the active ministry, although he remained senior minister until his death nine years later, on November 14, 1835. Greenwood became sole minister in 1835 and so continued until his death in 1843, when he lost his long battle with tuberculosis, the devastating disease and terrible killer of the nineteenth century.

Greenwood was recognized by his alma mater in 1839 when he received from Harvard the honorary degree of Doctor of Divinity. It was clear indication of the position he had achieved as a leading figure in the church life of his time. His reputation as minister is summarized in the memorial erected to him after his death and which stands on the left wall of the chancel in King's Chapel today. It is surely a moving tribute:

REV. FRANCIS WILLIAM PITT GREENWOOD, D.D.

The Colleague and Successor of Dr. Freeman as Pastor of this Church. Chosen July 11, 1824. Settled Aug. 29, 1824. Died Aug. 2, 1843. Aged 46 years.

Endowed with rare powers of observation and expression,
    his services in the pulpit were distinguished
    for their beauty, truth and persuasiveness.
The natural earnestness of his manner left no doubt of his
    sincerity;
the justness of his thoughts no room for censure;
and the poetical beauty of his language no objection.
His character, as developed through long years of
    lingering disease,
corresponds with that of his writings;
it was truly Christian, consistent, and attractive.

His people have placed this bust here in affectionate commemoration of his wisdom and his virtues. March, 1845.

The impression of a remarkable personality and character is constant wherever we find some account of Greenwood. But where are his letters, diaries, journals? Were they preserved? We have a substantial volume of his printed writings, but of his papers and unpublished records we have nothing. His marriage, family, private interests and thoughts, even his friendships—all are hidden from us.

As a preacher he was eloquent and impressive. Reading his *Sermons on Christian Consolations*, I find an engaging style as he comes to terms with themes of immortality and the inevitability of death, without any trace at all of morbidity, but rather with a powerful affirmation of Christian hope. His *Sermons to Children* are delightful. Take, for example, Sermon X, "Faults of Children," which is a candid statement about some characteristic traits to be found in children. He is not sentimental.

> Some children are obedient to those whom they ought to obey, and some are disobedient. . . . Some speak the truth always, and some speak a great deal of falsehood. . . . I am not one of those who think that children have no faults. I love children . . . but I remember what children were when I was a child, and I see what they are now; and I know that they have faults. Indeed, it would be a wonder if they had not.[6]

Then he speaks to his young listeners of several common faults, devoting two pages to willfulness, followed by a page and a half directed to the propensity of some children to disturb by teasing. Finally there is a short discourse on the subject of bullying, "a fault, or I should rather call it a sin . . . [is the] habit of tyrannizing over inferiors in age or strength." In the space of a page he makes clear the point that bullying is a despicable habit. Greenwood concluded on a fine pastoral note:

> And here I will stop, not because I have got through the list of the faults of children, but . . . I have already said enough for your attention and your memory. . . . Go on,

my children, from weakness to strength . . . and may the
good Spirit of God our Father go with you and help you.[7]

In 1835 he organized King's Chapel's first Sunday school, a
somewhat advanced idea for the time when we remember that
the Unitarian Sunday School Society had been organized only
eight years earlier in 1827.

Greenwood's sermons contained a genuine spirituality—
some called them mystical—and were truly catholic in spirit
and pastoral in tone. They were totally without sectarian
stamp, an important indication of his particular brand of liber-
alism. He had a high Christology, and he wanted to see a cross
in the church. It took another generation for that to happen.
During Dr. Greenwood's long periods of enforced confine-
ment in his battle with tuberculosis, he carved crosses, a
sample of which is the charming one to be seen in the church
Vestry. He declared, "Without Christ we can do nothing,
nothing in the concerns and ways of our highest life."[8]

Given the always problematic state of Greenwood's health,
and the fact that he had the sole responsibility of the ministry
of King's Chapel for most of his incumbency, I am impressed
with the range of his involvement in activities beyond the
boundaries of his parish. While in Baltimore he had edited
The Unitarian Miscellany, a short-lived but respected magazine, intended to provide a vehicle for liberal Christian ideas
and discussion. In 1821, The Christian Register began its long
history, ending with the merger of the American Unitarian
Association and the Universalist Church of America in 1961.
Greenwood was an early and frequent contributor to its col-
umns. Then there was the very distinguished Christian Examiner which gained national recognition as a journal of serious
theological thought and religious dialogue. Greenwood was
associate editor from 1831 until 1839 together with James
Walker who was president of Harvard College and president
of the Unitarian Association. Under the editorship of Greenwood and Walker that publication became the organ of the
higher intellectual life of the Unitarians and gave expression to
their interest in literature, general culture, and philanthropies,

as well as theological knowledge, but it was theological only in the broadest spirit.[9]

Greenwood stood quite apart from those who were attracted to the notions of Emerson and the movement that would come to be called "transcendentalism." Commenting on an unsigned review in *The Christian Examiner* attributed to Greenwood, William Hutchison writes: "The reviewer began by assuring readers that he was taking note of Emerson's 'strange notions' solely because the community desired to know whether or not most Unitarians considered Emerson's theories, 'so far as they are intelligible . . . to be neither good divinity nor good sense.' "[10] Greenwood's critical views were sharp, and his aim certain.

The Divinity School was founded in 1816 by an initial subscription of $30,000 under the auspices of the newly formed Society for the Promotion of Theological Education in Harvard University. Although a Unitarian effort from its beginning, it represented the nonsectarian sentiments of those nurturing it. This is evidenced by the sentence contained within the school's Act of Incorporation: ". . . and provided, also, that no assent to the peculiarities of any denomination of Christians shall be required of the beneficiaries of said Society; and that no discouragement be, in any manner or form, given to the serious, impartial, and unbiased investigation of Christian truth."

Greenwood served as the Society's secretary from 1831 to 1835. His role in the work of the Society is only one indication of his support for the Divinity School throughout his ministry. He was especially concerned with the development of the library and with the aid of needy divinity students, always in good supply. Both the library and student aid were regular items in the lists of King's Chapel's benevolences.

Greenwood made outstanding contributions to the life of the Unitarian churches by his presence on denominational boards and by his extensive writings and editing of materials for use in their churches. Another aspect of Greenwood's ministry that deserves notice is his social concern, demonstrated by the support of the work of the Ministry at Large

(forerunner to the Benevolent Fraternity) and the establishment of the Pitts Street Chapel, a special missionary effort for
King's Chapel. His proposal for the establishment of a fund for
religious and philanthropic uses appears to be the forerunner
of the Ministers Discretionary Fund and, perhaps, of the
present Charities and Appeals Committee. At his suggestion a
special Easter offering and the collections taken at Christmas
and at Communions were used for this purpose.[11]

In 1830 Greenwood's *Collection of Psalms and Hymns for
Christian Worship*, a substantial hymnal of some 560 selections,
was published. It was widely used until well into the latter half
of the nineteenth century, going through some fifty editions.
It was noteworthy in the fact that it introduced many modern
hymns. The hymns of Montgomery (six of them), Auber, four
by Bowring, three by Heber, and five by Charles Wesley
represented the work of authors whose hymns had not before
appeared in Unitarian collections. Emerson preached a sermon on hymns in 1831 in which he urged the Second Church
in Boston to adopt Greenwood's collection instead of that of
Jeremy Belknap. Writing in his journal in 1847, Emerson
declared that Greenwood's hymnal was still the best to be had.

Before Greenwood, Freeman had produced a collection of
hymns; this was a tradition that would be continued at King's
Chapel during the ministry of Henry Wilder Foote (1861-
1889). One might recall the wise words that serve as an epi-
graph in the 1937 *Hymns of the Spirit*: "In the hymn-book is the
true key to the doctrine of the communion of saints; for here
the saintly ones of all ages meet in their saintliest mood."

As with the great majority of the older parishes in Massachusetts, King's Chapel never took any formal action to affili-
ate with the American Unitarian Association. The church was
an independent church, conscious of its unique history and
character, aware that its Anglican roots and liturgical practice
set it apart from the churches around it. It had, certainly, never
been a Congregational church of the New England Way.
Excluded from the lists of Episcopal churches, it cherished its
independence while at the same time finding itself attached to
that body of liberal Christian churches that had thrust upon

them, before they ever chose it themselves, the name "Unitarian." The years from 1824 to 1843, spanning the last decade of Freeman's life and including the second decade of Greenwood's ministry, saw King's Chapel acquiring a Unitarian identity without diminishing in any way the sense of its singularity. The impression from every side is of a piece regarding Greenwood's spirit: He was not partisan in matters of theology, but he "... was earnest in the support of liberal Christianity, and with his Parish took part in the organization of various Unitarian associations which were formed in the early years of his ministry."[12]

In 1828 he told his congregation that it had seemed appropriate that the church, long under the care of James Freeman, "the venerable man who may be called the father of Unitarian Christianity in this country should do something for the cause long its own, especially when other churches of the same faith, much more lately vowed, were coming forward on all sides in aid of pure and simple religion."[13]

Nevertheless, because he recognized the damage caused by the growing theological dissension within the Unitarian ranks, he urged that King's Chapel not participate in councils called to settle controversies within and among the churches. Vestry records note his argument that it seemed expedient that King's Chapel separate itself from the other Unitarian churches in these matters. Within two years there was a further notation of a vote that the Wardens "be respectfully instructed to decline attendance at an ordination council."[14] Thus, through the years have the subtle lines of independence and association been sustained.

Greenwood's death followed that of William Ellery Channing within two years. His life and ministry were characterized by a deep spirituality that left its imprint on the life of the congregation he had served for two decades. In ways not yet fully articulated, he helped give shape to that special piety that came to be identified with Channing Unitarianism. Too little known, it nevertheless remains one of the sources of spirituality within the American experience.

Ephraim Peabody was born in Wilton, New Hampshire in

1807. He graduated from Bowdoin College and prepared for the ministry at the Harvard Divinity School. He was later to be honored by Harvard with the degree of Doctor of Divinity. His first ministry was in Meadville, Pennsylvania, in 1830. The next year he embarked upon missionary work in Cincinnati, and thus ensued four years filled with activities that included preaching, writing, traveling, and taking a full part in the busy life of that new city on the western frontier. They were exhilarating times for Peabody and his young wife.[15]

Peabody's powers as a preacher were not inconsiderable. Harriet Martineau, the English journalist and traveler (who was not known for lavish praise), told in her account of her American tour of getting to know the Peabodys in Cincinnati. She found Ephraim Peabody ". . . to be loved, fervently but rationally, by his flock, some of whom think him not a whit inferior as a preacher, to Dr. Channing."[16]

Then came an ominous first bout with tuberculosis, the disease from which he would never fully recover. Two winters in Mobile, Alabama, brought improvement to his health, and his preaching there resulted in the establishment of a Unitarian church. The following summer he filled the pulpit of the Federal Street Church in Boston, and then accepted a call to join with the Reverend John Morison in an associate ministry in New Bedford where he remained for eight happy and fruitful years.

In 1845 Ephraim Peabody was invited to become minister of King's Chapel. It was a difficult decision, not least because of his health. Eventually he decided to accept the challenge. Perhaps, he thought, he had another ten years to live! He was right; the Peabody years were from 1846 to 1856.

The demands of his pastoral ministry were heavy from the beginning, undoubtedly because that had been most wanting in Greenwood's last years. The church school was a priority, and he quickly became engaged in the liturgical life of the church for which he obviously had a deep appreciation. His efforts in providing for the instruction of the children resulted in a carefully prepared curriculum of study based on clearly articulated principles, which he set forth in his plan entitled

"Christian Instruction in the Church."

The object of religious education, he said, was ". . . to train up a child as a Christian from the beginning."[17] His interest and concern for religious education extended over and beyond the limits of his own congregation. He was involved in the Sunday school societies that were springing up, and he contributed to what may have been the first graded series of church school texts, published in 1852. Peabody wrote the volume on the Old Testament.[18]

Peabody's ministry was marked by a deep involvement in social action. He was a close friend and ally of Joseph Tuckerman, himself a member of King's Chapel, in Tuckerman's many efforts in urban ministry. Peabody was more able than Tuckerman in dealing with social concerns, and he had real skill in matters of organization. He was a pivotal figure in the evening school at Pitts Street Chapel, one of the early social ministries supported by King's Chapel and a number of other Boston Unitarian churches. He wrote and talked about the social problem of poverty and was a staunch and effective proponent of vocational education in the public schools. He was active in adult education, especially among the large number of immigrants arriving in Boston in the middle decades of the nineteenth century. George Willis Cooke acknowledged Peabody's singular contributions in ministering to the poor when he wrote: "It is well to notice the efforts of one man, because his work led to the scientific methods of charitable relief which are employed in Boston at the present time."[19]

Joseph Tuckerman had tried to organize the diverse charitable efforts that were being carried on in the city, but there was duplication resulting in wasted effort and resources. Ephraim Peabody with his keen sense of organization came to the rescue; the result was the founding of the Boston Provident Association. The Association was organized by dividing Boston into districts, each with its own head, thus enabling careful planning and neighborhood participation. The Provident Association became in 1879 the Associated Charities of Boston. One can continue to document Peabody's influence in the organizing of the Fragment Society, the Children's Mission, and in the work of the Benevolent Fraternity of Unitarian Churches. In all of these undertakings he had the support of his congregation; he was the catalyst as well in rallying support for urban ministries and social action among Unitarians throughout the city.

I have been attempting to trace the story of how King's Chapel became involved in the life of the Unitarian churches. Peabody continued to be identified with Unitarian causes as had Greenwood and Freeman before him, thus drawing King's Chapel into that larger association of liberal churches. Ephraim Peabody's denominational activities were not inconsiderable. In 1852 he was breaking new ground in editing the eight-volume graded series of religious education manuals to which I have already referred.

For several years Peabody was editor of *The Christian Register*, and he was an active contributor to the *North American Review* as well. He wrote several pamphlets issued and distributed by the American Unitarian Association, including one entitled "Come Over and Help Us" (Boston, 1855), in which he addressed the matter of the missionary responsibilities of the liberal churches. This may serve as a useful reminder to contemporary readers that there are, indeed, some forgotten aspects of our heritage. In any case, one is reminded of Peabody's commitment to missionary activity in the west and south in the early days of his own ministry.[20]

No account of Peabody would be complete without some mention of his attitude toward the great moral issue of his day. Ephraim Peabody was in every way opposed to slavery. He had shown his commitment to acting on behalf of slaves years before in Cincinnati when he had befriended and assisted Frederick Douglass. He knew well enough the effect of the evils of slavery on white and black alike. In his response to Daniel Webster's famous speech of March 7, 1850, he declared that ". . . the master is as much fettered to one end of the chain as the slave is to the other. . . . There is not one moral or social interest which does not feel its disastrous influence."[21]

He saw the sense in Webster's argument that an immediate

emancipation of slaves by force would violate others' rights and certainly destroy the Union. Webster argued for a program of gradualism, building on the growth of emancipation sentiments in the south, the increased numbers of freed slaves, and various proposals for colonization of former slaves in Jamaica and Africa. Sharing Webster's fears for an embattled Union, Peabody said the alternative to a gradual and planned emancipation was disunion, which was tantamount to "breaking up a noble ship that the crew might find greater safety on rafts constructed out of fragments."[22]

His quiet, reasoned views were not well received by louder voices calling for dissolution. Friends were divided. Theodore Parker was surely the most uncivil of all those calling for radical solutions when he referred to Peabody as "the spaniel of King's Chapel." Henry Wilder Foote, the editor of the *Annals*, referring to this episode, says that Parker's reputation suffered more than Peabody's in the long run.[23] Samuel Gridley Howe wrote to Parker: "Dear Parker, you overrate things; you are childish about some matters of commonsense . . . [You have] a besetting sin, in which some of your friends encourage you—uncharitableness of thought and word."[24]

Ephraim Peabody made no attempt to defend himself; he continued to work for and with runaway slaves within the context of his own ministry. He advised and befriended "Father Henson," a fugitive slave who worked for a colony of escaped slaves in Canada. Father Henson was often a guest in the Peabody home, and a familiar figure at Morning Prayer in King's Chapel and at the altar rail for communion whenever possible. There could, I think, be no stronger evidence of Peabody's commitment to working for the eradication of the curse of slavery in America than is to be seen in the friendship of these two men.

Ephraim Peabody was conservative in the right ways. He was absolutely clear in his conviction that politics should be kept out of the pulpit. That was not the place to discuss how a vote should be cast. He was criticized, and the criticism hurt, but he held firm. Who is there, he asked, that needed to use the pulpit to say what he had to say? Yet he knew that Christian conscience demanded response and action to the moral issues of the moment.

His vision for the larger ministry to the new urban poor, his work for educational reform, his efforts on behalf of fugitive slaves—all these endeavors bear the stamp of a compassionate and creative ministry. One can understand the feelings that prompted the words that are inscribed on the pedestal of his memorial bust that stands at the right of the chancel in King's Chapel:

HIS COUNSELS AND HIS EXAMPLE WERE
ALIKE PERSUASIVE—
IF AFFECTION COULD HAVE KEPT HIM
WITH US,
HE HAD NOT DIED SO SOON.

Peabody's old friend and classmate from Divinity School days, George Parker, visited him during his last illness. It was by Parker that Ephraim Peabody sent a message of great power to his congregation: "Tell them to lean with entire confidence and unreserve on the authority of Christ as the revealer of God." Then looking at the cross on the opposite wall, he continued to speak: ". . . no theory of human life can stand which leaves out the cross!"[25]

The contributions of Freeman, Greenwood, and Peabody in liturgy and hymnody are known, but they are deserving of more penetrating contextual study than has yet been undertaken. Freeman was, of course, responsible for the first edition of the *Book of Common Prayer According to the Use in King's Chapel.* Francis Greenwood was responsible for the third, fourth, and fifth editions, and Peabody for the sixth. The modifications that each made to the preceding edition disclose a good deal about the personal theology and the changing sentiments of King's Chapel's ministers and its congregations, respectively, in the first seventy years of its history as a Unitarian church. The additions and, especially, the restorations are particularly noteworthy. In hymnody Greenwood's influence is distinctive. So far as I have been able to ascertain, he composed no hymns himself, but his much admired *Collection of Psalms and Hymns for Christian Worship,* first published in 1830, had passed through fifty-seven editions by 1853.[26]

James Freeman and Joseph May, Senior Warden for three decades, had published *Psalms and Hymns* in 1799, a hymnal for King's Chapel's use. At least one hymn by Freeman has maintained a place in our hymnbook and is still sung today. Peabody, too, wrote at least one hymn that was sung at ordinations and appeared in a distinguished hymnal edited by Frederick Henry Hedge and Frederic Dan Huntington in 1853, entitled *Hymns for The Church of Christ,* and said to be the finest hymnal of its day, more catholic than any of its predecessors.[27] In their work in liturgy and hymnody, these three shaped the language and forms of worship and praise not only for King's Chapel but for Christian worship in wider Unitarian circles.[28]

My task in this series has been to examine the experience of King's Chapel as it moved from its Anglican beginnings toward Unitarianism in the first half of the nineteenth century. I am struck by the harmony that prevailed in the congregation during the ministries of Freeman, Greenwood, and Peabody. This is all the more impressive when we remember the dissensions that troubled this same congregation during the colonial period.

After the American Revolution, King's Chapel became an independent congregation. Jealously guarding that dearly won independence, it nevertheless remained a continuing Christian presence in the community of liberal churches. In civic reform, in new patterns of urban ministry, in educational and philanthropic efforts, King's Chapel played an active role. It was in the best sense a conservative witness within a liberal denomination. It was an ecumenical witness, too, in a denomination that all too often found itself isolated by pestiferous sectarianism.

To capture the spirit of King's Chapel in the nineteenth century, and down to our own time, we cannot, I think, improve on Freeman's words, penned in his preface to the prayerbook of 1785: "Our earnest desire is to live in brotherly love and peace with all men, and especially with those who call themselves the disciples of Jesus Christ." It's not a bad tradition; it's a goodly heritage—we can be grateful for it.

Notes

1. For a fuller account of Unitarian beginnings see Charles C. Forman, "Elected Now By Time," in *A Stream of Light: A Short History of American Unitarianism*, ed. C. Conrad Wright (Boston: Unitarian Universalist Association, 1975), pp. 3-32.
2. I have discussed Buckminster more fully in the work cited above, pp. 12-16.
3. The Unitarian concern for biblical criticism is treated extensively in Jerry M. Brown, *The Rise of Biblical Criticism in America, 1800-1870* (Middletown, CT: Wesleyan University Press, 1969). See especially chapters 1, 2, 4, 5, 8, 10.
4. *King's Chapel Prayerbook* (Boston: Peter Edes, 1785), p. 246.
5. William B. Sprague, *Annals of the American Pulpit* (New York: Robert Carter and Brothers, 1865), Vol. *8*, p. 172.
6. Francis William Pitt Greenwood, *Sermons to Children* (Boston: James Munroe, 1841), p. 99.
7. *Ibid.*, p. 108.
8. Quoted in *An American Reformation. A Documentary History of Unitarian Christianity*, ed. Sydney Ahlstrom and Jonathan S. Carey (Middletown, CT: Wesleyan University Press, 1985), p. 146. Ahlstrom refers to "... a rich tradition of mystical spirituality that inspires the sermons and devotions of such men as Francis William Pitt Greenwood and Ephraim Peabody."
9. George Willis Cooke, *Unitarianism in America* (Boston: American Unitarian Association, 1910), p. 101.
10. William R. Hutchison, *The Transcendentalist Ministers: Church Reform in the New England Renaissance* (New Haven, CT: Yale University Press, 1959), p. 79.
11. *Annals of King's Chapel*, Vol. 2, eds. Henry Edes and Henry Wilder Foote (Boston: Little Brown, 1896) has a useful account of this aspect of King's Chapel's life during Francis Greenwood's ministry. See pp. 466-469.
12. *Ibid.*, p. 466.
13. *Ibid.*
14. *Cf.* Minutes from Vestry Records for March 25, 1841 and Dec. 30, 1842, cited in Edes and Foote, *Annals of King's Chapel*, Vol. 2, p. 467.
15. For a charming account of Ephraim and Mary Jane Peabody, see their sons' account in *A New England Romance* (Boston: Houghton Mifflin, 1920). Chapter 3, "An Itinerant Ministry," pp. 83 ff covers the Cincinnati years.
16. *Ibid.*, p. 93.

17. *Annals of King's Chapel*, eds. Edes and Foote, Vol. 2, pp. 524f.
18. George W. Cooke, *Unitarianism in America* (Boston: American Unitarian Association, 1910), pp. 262-272. For an important account of the rise and early history of Unitarian Sunday schools, see Lewis G. Pray, *History of Sunday Schools and of Religious Education from the Earliest Times* (Boston: Crosby and Nichols, 1847).
19. Cooke, *Unitarianism in America*, p. 334.
20. There is a large body of Peabody material yet to be examined in King's Chapel's archives as well as material in other collections awaiting study. It is certain that such an examination will confirm and substantiate Peabody's contribution to the life of the larger Unitarian community.
21. Quoted in Peabody and Peabody, *A New England Romance*, p. 124.
22. *Ibid.*, p. 125.
23. *Annals of King's Chapel*, eds. Edes and Foote, Vol. 2, p. 517.
24. This description of Peabody's stance in the period preceding the Civil War is taken from Peabody and Peabody, *A New England Romance*, pp. 123-130.
25. From the memorial sermon preached at King's Chapel on December 12, 1856 and cited in *Annals of King's Chapel*, eds. Edes and Foote, Vol. 2, p. 521.
26. William B. Sprague, *Annals of the American Pulpit*, Vol. 8 (New York: Robert Carter, 1965), p. 487. Henry Wilder Foote says of Greenwood's *Collection* that it was "the hymn-book most widely used in Unitarian churches in the first half of the 19th century." It was used at King's Chapel for sixty years. I am indebted for the information on hymnody contained in this chapter to the generosity of the late Dr. Foote. The work is an unpublished manuscript entitled *American Unitarian Hymn Writers and Hymns* compiled in 1959 by Henry Wilder Foote for the Hymn Society of America.
27. Peabody's hymn is entitled "Lift Aloud the Voice of Praise."
28. This tradition was continued and enriched by the work of Henry Wilder Foote, minister from 1861 to 1889. His ministry deserves careful study, a project that I hope to undertake in the near future.

Afterword

Our reason for publishing these essays is to set this critical chapter of King's Chapel's history in the larger context of American intellectual and ecclesiastical history and to show in particular how "American" was the reform at this church and how inevitable the division with its episcopally ordered parent.

There is another reason for reviewing in such detail the account of James Freeman's ordination. For over a century the basic source of information on this event has been Chapters 20 and 21 in Volume II of the *Annals of King's Chapel.* Recently, we have found reason to question the completeness of this account.

Not long ago Mrs. Nancy Kessner, then our church archivist, discovered in our archives a letter written by Henry Edes, editor of Volume II of the *Annals,* to the Senior Warden, Arthur Lyman. In this letter Mr. Edes tells Mr. Lyman that he asked a colleague, a Harvard professor, to write the chapters on Freeman. According to his letter, Mr. Edes culled from the material left to him by Henry Wilder Foote, editor of Volume I, three large bundles of relevant material as well as copious verbatim extracts, which Mr. Edes had made from the Parish and Vestry records. All these materials he turned over to his colleague.

When, however, the proofs of his colleague's chapters came to Mr. Edes, he found that he

had practically ignored all this original material, and after describing Dr. Freeman's ordination, the most important event in the theological history of the Chapel and events leading up to it, had cited the secondary authority of Dr. Greenwood's *History of King's Chapel.*

In consequence a great opportunity for writing a chapter of surpassing interest was lost! Moreover, the dear old Doctor made a number of very bad blunders in names, dates, and statements of fact which the Editor was compelled to correct, in some cases being obliged to destroy a whole electrolytic plate and to have the page reset and recast. Furthermore, . . . [he] destroyed—or, at least, did not return to me—the material I had sent to him, except a very small bundle which was of little value. The loss of this matter is deplorable because it was so voluminous, various and valuable."[1]

Mr. Edes then added, "These facts are for your own eye and ear only . . . since they concern one of my oldest, and dearest, and best friends, who has gone to his rich reward."[2]

Over ninety years have passed since the publication of this second volume of the *Annals*, and it seemed to us appropriate to let this lapse be known, especially since we hope through these two essays to encourage others to study the life and work of James Freeman more fully.

James Freeman deserves at least a monograph which might describe his life in more detail, including his associations in the city, his home in Newton, his efforts on behalf of Unitarianism, and his friends and family to whom he was devoted. Rich resources for such a monograph are available at the Houghton Library, the Massachusetts Historical Society, and of course the archives of King's Chapel at the parish house.

Another monograph might compare the liturgical revisions of Samuel Clarke, Theophilus Lindsey, and James Freeman, perhaps showing the possible influence of Clarke's work on the proposed American Episcopalian prayerbook of 1785. The ambitious scholar might explore the liturgical innovations conducted by "the rational Anglicans" in England during the 1700s. *Worship and Theology in England* by Horton Davies,[3] *The Making of the First American Prayerbook* (Chapter 2) by Marion Hatchett,[4] and *A History of Anglican Liturgy* (Chapter 8) by G.J. Cummings[5] will provide an introduction to this rich and largely unexplored domain.

As suggested in Chapter 4, Francis William Pitt Greenwood, Ephraim Peabody, and Henry Wilder Foote are deserving of scholarly investigation. Their ministries have been chronicled in the *Annals of King's Chapel*, but a large body of materials exists in the archives of the Andover-Harvard Library, the Massachusetts Historical Society, and at King's Chapel for Peabody and Foote. In the absence of archival material for Greenwood, a careful study of his published writings is surely desirable. Such an investigation would be a valuable addition to a seriously neglected aspect of Unitarian history.

In conclusion, Carl Scovel wishes to thank Pamela Barz, his friend and former Ministerial Assistant, who did much of the substantial research for these papers and thus enabled him to draw some of his conclusions.

We wish also to thank the Minns Lectureship Committee for their kind invitation to deliver these lectures and for the opportunity to gather into these four lectures hitherto scattered thoughts and observations.

Notes

1. Henry Edes to Arthur Lyman, September 27, 1897, Archives of King's Chapel at the Parish House.
2. *Ibid.*
3. Horton Davies, *Worship and Theology in England, from Watts and Wesley to Maurice, 1690-1850* (Princeton, NJ: Princeton University Press, 1975).
4. Marion Hatchett, "The Making of the First American Prayerbook," submitted in partial fulfillment of the requirements for the degree of Doctor of Theology in the General Theological Seminary, New York City, February 1, 1972.

5. G.J. Cummings, *A History of Anglican Liturgy* (London: MacMillan, 1982).

The Minns Lectures

The Minns Lectures were established by Miss Susan Minns of Boston in honor of her brother, Thomas Minns.

He was a descendant of two of the Colonial clergy: John Wilson, the first minister of First Church in Boston, and the Rev. Thomas Hooker. Minns was born in New York City in 1833, but the family soon moved to the Boston area. He was a commission merchant for many years, a leader in the milling industry, and active in building the railways in the West. He was community minded, being one of the founders of the Museum of Fine Arts; a trustee of the Boston Athenaeum; and a member of the Colonial Society of Massachusetts, the Massachusetts Historical Society, and the Bostonian Society. A member of King's Chapel, he was also active in the Society for Ministerial Relief and the Society for Propagating the Gospel Among the Indians and Others in North America. He was noted for his sterling integrity, unremitting diligence, and sound judgment. He died in 1913.

Susan Minns was the oldest alumna of Massachusetts Institute of Technology when she died in 1938. She was a scientist, art collector, and philanthropist. She had been active in furthering the cause of women's education and was a botanist and biologist of note. She donated a mountain to the Commonwealth. Called Little Wachusett, it is located in Princeton and reserved as a bird sanctuary.

The Minns Lectures are administered by a joint committee of members from First and Second Church in Boston and King's Chapel. Miss Minns wanted the lectures to address religion or religious subjects and to be delivered by Unitarian Universalist ministers in good standing.

A Roster of Lectures

1992   Ed Lynn: *The Shape of Worship: The Unitarian Universalist Search for the Embodiment of the Spiritual*

1991   Neil Schadle: *The Liberal Church as a Theater of Democracy*

       Max Gaebler: *Unitarianism in Britain, America, and Australasia: A Study in Contrasts*

1990   Carl Seaburg: *Inventing a Ministry*

1989   Charles Forman and Carl Scovel: *A Journey Toward Independence*

1988   Eric A. Haugan: *James Luther Adams and Liberation Theology*

1987   Erwin Gaede: *The Myth of the Medical Model*

1987   Khoren Arisian: *Humanism and the Spirituality of the Future*

1987   Homer A. Jack: *Nuclear Politics After Hiroshima/Nagasaki—Unitarian Universalist and Other Responses*

1986   John Nichols: *Liberal Religion's Response to Loss*

1986   Rhys Williams: *A Time to Stress Unity*

1985   Philip Zwerling: *Rituals of Oppression—Anti-Communism and the Liberal Church*

1984   F. Forrester Church: *Paradox and the Poetry of God*

1984   Earl Holt III: *Unitarianism in St. Louis 1834-1887: The Life and Times of William Greenleaf Eliot*

1983   Victor H. Carpenter: *The Black Empowerment Controversy and the Unitarian Universalist Association*

1982   John Erdo: *The Rise of Unitarianism in Transylvania*

1981   John Ruskin Clark: *A Prophet Not Without Honor: Joseph Priestley*

1980   V. Emil Gudmundson: *Icelandic Unitarianism in North America*

1980   Joseph A. Bassett: *Vatican II and the New England Way*

1979   Charles C. Forman: *Faith and Story*

1978   Duncan Howlett: *The Critical Way in Religion*

1977   Doris Hunter: *The Utopian Vision and American Liberal Religion: A Dialogue*

1976   Carl Scovel: *The Christian Resistance in Nazi Germany*

1975   Harry Hoehler: *Christian Responses to Other Faiths*

1975   Virgil E. Murdock: *The Institutional History of the American Unitarian Association*

1974   Prescott B. Wintersteen: *The Life, Death, and Resurrection of Jesus Christ in American Unitarianism*

1972   Phillip Hewett: *Racovia: The Unitarian Search for Community in Sixteenth-Century Poland*

1971   Donald S. Harrington: *The Firestorm of Scientific and Technological Change*

1970   Walter Donald Kring: *American Mystics*

1969   John MacLaughlan: *Humanism in the Christian Tradition*

1968/69   Wallace Bush: *Religion and Modern Literature*

1968   Harry H. Hoehler: *Encounter with the World's Faiths*

1967   Ralph N. Helverson: *The Human City*

1966   John W. Cyrus: *On the Liberal Ministry*

1965   George Hunston Williams: *Changing Patterns in the Christian Understanding of Other Religions*

1964   Jack Mendelsohn: *That the Light May Not Fail*

1963   Lancelot A. Garrard: *Athens or Jerusalem*

1962   Seth R. Brooks: *Religion in Three Dimensions*

1962   Dorothy Tilden Spoerl: *Creativity*

1961   Wallace Robbins: *The Natural Power of the Christian Myth*

1961   H. Stewart Carter: *The Psychological Aspects of Religion*

1960   John F. Hayward: *Existentialism and Religious Affirmation*

1959   Arthur Foote: *The Impact of Freud upon Religion and Morality*

1959 John Kielty: *British Unitarianism—Past, Present, Future*

1958 Floyd Ross: *Man, Myth, and Maturity*

1958 Robert T. Weston: *Worship for a Free Church*

1957 Jacob Trapp: *The Inward Way*

1956 Joseph Barth: *Toward a Doctrine of the Liberal Church*

1955 Dana McLean Greeley: *Personal Social Action*

1955 Robert Storer: *The Promise of Inner Peace*

1955 Malcolm R. Sutherland, Jr.: *The Possibilities of Happiness*

1954 Palfrey Perkins: *Christian Simplicities*

1953 Frederick May Eliot: *The Practice of Preaching*

1952 Leslie T. Pennington: *The Disciplines of Liberty*

1951 Charles E. Park: *The Way of Jesus*

1950 James Luther Adams: *Protestantism and the Patterns of Power*

1949 Alexander St. Ivanyi: *Underground Christianity*

1948 Von Ogden Vogt: *Religion and American Culture*

1947 Frank O. Holmes: *Unitarians as Members of a Worshipping Community*

1947 Charles E. Park: *Christianity*

1946 Alexander Winston: *Jesus, Lord of Life*

1946 Harry Meserve and Arthur Foote: *The Theist's Answer and the Inclusive Answer*

1946 J. A. C. Fagginger Auer: *God: A Vital Question for the Humanist's Answer*

1945 Duncan Howlett: *The Liberal Movement in Religion*

1945 Joseph H. Giunta, Howard Brooks, and Stephen H. Fritchman: *Religion, War, and the Work of the Unitarian Service Committee*

1944 Earl Davis, John H. Lothrop, and Norman D. Fletcher: *Modern Christianity at Work*

1944 Edwin Slacombe: *Seeking and Finding God*

1943/44 Herbert Hitchen: *The Religious Element in Contemporary Poetry*

1943 A. Powell Davies: *The Struggle for the Mind of America*

1942 Walton E. Cole: *Realistic Courage*